For my son Luke and my best friend Luke.
May God stir your hearts and make you leaders of men.

And for my three brothers.

BREATHING IN
AND
BREATHING OUT

Leader of Men

JOHN-PETER DEMSICK

IRON MAST PUBLISHING

Copyright © 2013 by John-Peter Demsick

All rights reserved. Written permission must be secured from the publisher to use or reproduce any part of this book, except for brief quotations in reviews or articles.

Published in Vero Beach, Florida by Iron Mast Publishing.

Front cover photo courtesy of Terry & Sarah Photography at www.terryandsarahphotography.com.

Unless otherwise noted, Scripture quotations are from the HOLY BIBLE: NEW INTERNATIONAL VERSION®. Copyright © 1973, 1978, 1984 by International Bible Society.

Scripture quotations noted NASB are from the NEW AMERICAN STANDARD BIBLE. Copyright © 1960, 1995 by the Lockman Foundation.

Scripture quotations noted KJV are from THE KING JAMES VERSION. Copyright © 1979, 1980, 1982, 1990, 1994 by Thomas Nelson, Inc.

Scripture quotations noted NKJV are from THE NEW KING JAMES VERSION. Copyright © 1979, 1980, 1982 by Thomas Nelson, Inc.

ISBN 0-9892-4780-5

Printed in the United States of America.

CONTENTS

Chapter 1—The Modern Day Church..................................1
Chapter 2—Masculinity...15
Chapter 3—A Boy's Battles..29
Chapter 4—Femininity..42
Chapter 5—The Thread...52
Chapter 6—Breathing In and Breathing Out.....................63
Chapter 7—Identity Crisis in Church...............................78
---- The Pastor----
Chapter 8—Stirring the Bride..88
        (Preparing His Heart)
Chapter 9—Locked in Little Treasure Chests...................102
        (Listening and Assessing)
Chapter 10—The Team Coach..113
        (Discipling)
Chapter 11—The Oak and Its Sprinkler System...............128
        (Relationships with God)
Chapter 12—Love In Champagne Bottles........................142
        (Family Relationships)
----The Church ----
Chapter 13—Captain at the Helm...................................155
Chapter 14—Exponentiating the Kingdom......................164
Chapter 15—Leader of Men..181

INTRODUCTION

Years ago, a friend Terry, my brother Richard, and I led a Christian club at the local public high school. After some discussion, we tried a bold move—we had the students lead everything. They planned meetings, gave talks, and led prayers. Surprisingly, far more students showed up wanting to lead than to participate.

And in one of those moments when you recall someone beckoning you over and uttering a secret that has since changed your life, Terry leaned in and whispered a statement that stuck with me.

"When natural leaders walk into a place where there are no opportunities to lead, they naturally leave."

I have never been able to shake it.

That is what has happened with the church.

Breathing In and Breathing Out

Leader of Men

-Chapter One-

THE MODERN DAY CHURCH

Men don't belong in church.

As I sit in the cove of my back porch, watching the white pines sway and toss before me, gusts showering small, dart-like missiles in surging waves across my lawn, I huddle into my chair a little deeper. Wind howls through the trees as a siren begins to wail in the distance, reminding that danger lurks out in the vast beyond. Overly aggressive fronts spatter across and into my hiding place, chilling me with cold, hard pellets of water. Impending dark clouds loom in the sky, warning with an occasional menacing boom of their approach. The Florida treasure coast has come alive with a fury that must have once sent the fiercest Seminole scurrying for cover.

I should probably be inside. That is precisely the reason I'm out here.

The deep forest that butts up against my house holds something majestic that beckons me. Perhaps it is mystery of the unknown. Today, perhaps, it is a conquest that reflects a battle within. A battle at this moment I'm winning, as I hunker down and take the brute force of the storm. At times like these, it calls in a way no magnitude of wetness or warning of danger can prevent.

I was born to be here at this moment.

I was born to live free, no, to *live or die* in a great conquest, a sweeping story. However, my conquest may not be found underneath palmetto brush or in deep woods padded with beds of pine needles. I may be inspired there. But they can never keep me, not longer than the awe of exploring or rush of the outdoors, which wear thin. No, what I sense runs deeper. Something this raging wild before me reminds me of. Awesome and powerful, breathtaking yet surreal, it captures the fierceness of scores of warriors lined up for a combative rush yet the picturesque beauty of a Bride breathlessly awaiting a wedding day.

And I'm sure of it now.

Something more than me, my blanket, my chair, and the wild lingers out here in the cold. Something demanding a response. More than a feeling, it is an ache, a desire or...*calling*.

Perhaps that's what I've found out here in the storm, as the heavens pelt away at me with friendly fire, whilst I curl up under the safety of my little hideaway. A calling from within that was written on my heart since boyhood but etched in the stars long before.

One so epic it becomes holy.

A calling that leads me to the church.

A DIFFERENT SETTING

But men don't belong in church.

As I sit staring ahead, listening to the sermon, pondering the back of the person's head in front of me, while he is pondering the back of the person's head in front of him, I wonder how we got here. I mean, I got here by way of the parking lot. A smiling man in an orange vest, no doubt cautious of the dangers of reckless, late church-goers competing with time on natural grass turf, waved me in.

And I slid into my spot.

So now I'm here.

But, I have to admit, not much more thought was put into it. And I'll add, for the majority of us, not much more will be. We're not lazy, worthless bums or lumps of creamer-fed donut fat, although if we're lucky we rolled through the local donut shop drive thru (without stopping) and filled up on our weekly ration of double chocolate glazed before we arrived. Late.

We're good men. We saved halves of cream cheesed bagels for our wives and iced coffees to get them through the struggle of wriggling the kids to Sunday School.

Oh, yeah. And I almost forgot. I *did* my manly duty this morning. I picked out the family pew seat.

And I slid into my spot.

Not much more has been asked of me, and if I stick around, I have a feeling probably not much more will be.

You see, I'm in church.

And, like I said, men don't belong in church.

THE DILEMMA

Now, I don't mean men shouldn't be in church, but that there is no place for them. Not in the current church.

Let me explain. Guys throughout time have longed to fight, to strategize, to lead. *To embark.* To accept a top secret mission. We dream about jumping in front of bullets or kicking through walls and shooting bad guys who threaten lives of damsels in distress, who in turn fall madly in love with us as we gingerly sweep them off their feet. Without breaking a sweat (or an appendage). And *without* a post-rampage chiropractic appointment. We want something real. Like that. Well, make-believe real, anyway. Something with action and feet sweeping.

Really, we want an exciting mission that's romantic. Life or death. The stakes raised. The future resting on us.

And that's how we feel about church, too. Give us that kind of call, and we're all in. Set us along the wall with a stack of service bulletins and a hello name tag and we're…unimpressed.

So what does that mean for men? Where does it leave us now?

Well, in the pages that follow, this book will unveil the simple, clear call of God on every man. It will reveal, through his design, that God has a plan, and the patterns we see in nature, the desires that stir deeply in our hearts, he intended to fulfill a crucial purpose. *In every man.* That means every man has a purpose in the church. It means you do. If true, this will have revolutionary implications.

If man's nature is unique, if he was formed with a specific design—a blueprint, perhaps—of strength, initiative, and leadership at creation, then the church needs to change to match that. Not the other way around. In this culture, we often ask men to change to fit the church. Follow the rules, be quiet, fold your hands, find your pew, and please sit down. Or as I was once asked—*if you're going to dance while worshiping, please stand in the back. We don't want you to distract anyone.* When I politely mentioned David dancing before the Lord, I was told I would be welcome to find another church.

Well, this isn't a book about dancing. It isn't about styles of worship, the top ten rules of how not to rock the half-submerged boat, or why fitting in is better than standing up. It is a book about men. It is about exactly *who* we are. But because it's about men, it's also about the church. The two are inseparable; one flows naturally out of the other.

And the only way for the church to meet its true purpose is to fulfill the purpose of every person in it.

To empower them in Christ, as men and as women. That is discipleship.

But where does that leave us now? Unfortunately, as I think you'll see, it's not very far.

THE STATE OF THE CHURCH

In most churches, one man leads. One has the authority. One man gives the vision. One makes the decisions for direction and financial stewardship. And, usually, one man gives the sermons and ministers to the people.

All of those men are the pastor. Find a church in which the senior pastor disciples others to preach and step up as leaders more than doing it himself, and you'll have found a rare church. I haven't seen one. Rather, the pastor usually sees preaching and teaching as his primary job. It's what he's being paid for, right? But when one puts together all the responsibilities of preaching, teaching, setting vision, managing staff and volunteers, decision-making, visiting hospitals, leading the midweek Bible study, giving announcements, resolving conflicts, and so many other leadership tasks that make up "exercising the authority" in the church, it usually becomes clear there is a massive burden on one man. And it's not the guy with the donut bag in the back row who's suspiciously staring at the back of the person's head in front of him.

It's the pastor.

Of course, there are other forms of church leadership—elderships, presbyteries, and boards—that balance authority with the pastor. But even in those leadership plans, it's common to have the bulk of responsibilities fall on that one man.

This isn't a problem for women. That may be a strange transition. But think about it for a moment. It is natural for women to attach to a godly man. Their natures perfectly complement a male leader. They're used to sitting under a man's teaching and leadership. At the heart of it all is submission, following the lead.

Now the point should become clear. Women were designed to beautifully function as a support while following a proper lead, a head. Therefore, today's church has the perfect structure *for women*. Women feel comfortable following the one man who, in a practical way, is leading the church. It's natural, like breathing in and breathing out.

Serving, listening, receiving, adapting beliefs to the pastor's ministry of the Word—everything it is to be a modern-day congregant—is natural to them. It is the very role God designed for them in the family and an easy transition.

But there's a problem. Men were designed to *be* the head, to lead. It is their inherent nature. In a healthy man, apart from the world's manipulation, it is completely natural.

Like breathing in and breathing out.

So how do men fit in the church? Like I said, they don't. Sure they're *supposed* to learn, serve, submit to leadership, and be involved. But how do they best fit? Simple. They fit by living out their God-given nature in the church just as anywhere else.

They're supposed to lead.

But when one observes the modern-day church and men, there's something missing from this picture.

THE ABSENCE OF MEN

In most churches, sadly, the men just aren't there. They see no significant role in church. Sure, some serve as elders or ushers. Some play on worship teams or teach Sunday School classes. But the vast majority do nothing. And many more aren't there at all.

It is as though a whole generation of men walked into the church, saw no place for themselves, and quietly walked out.

They did not belong, and they knew it.

Where is the place for the man who is inspired by vision and purpose, who is motivated by a greater cause? He dreams of battles and heroic fantasies. He loves strategizing over anything from Axis and Allies to luring the elusive red fish, restoring his father's '66 Mustang, or positioning his son's Little League team for the pennant. Heck, my brother has probably spent more time dissecting and analyzing the Detroit Pistons and their paths to success than their general manager, Joe Dumars, has.

Even a man's job offers him the validation of increased position, responsibility, and respect.

When the church invites him to share a pew and sit humbly, how can it ever compete with that?

Quite simply, it can't.

And that's why he's not there.

Sure, he'll bring his family now and then for the Sunday School. And he thinks of himself as a man who loves God. But there is no connection between his internal desires and his place in the church.

Every week he goes, he knows it. Not consciously, just at the place in his heart where he decides to dutifully attend for his family but will hash over every factor of whether the Jets can beat the Packers on Sunday night.

It's not really his fault. He isn't irresponsible. He puts significant time into living out his nature in the venues he's given, pushing for deadlines at work and analyzing and coaching the Broncos on Sunday.

He just doesn't do this in church.

That's because it's not an exciting mission inviting him in. When he goes to church, there's no place for his heart, his nature. With no opportunity for the armchair tactician or business visionary, he becomes a distant face in the pew. He knows it's important, but there's no place that's right *for him*.

What he misses is he is irreplaceable. It's the most exciting mission a man can take. He has a role he must fill. Like William Wallace in *Braveheart*, if he doesn't lead his troops, there will be no storming of Stirling. No victory at Bannockburn. The tactician, the coach, the team or business visionary, all fit perfectly in the church God designed. Only, it isn't the church that exists today. So he does not see it, and he slips off into other passions that better fit his make-up. That is the tragedy. And it is the church's fault.

The current church leaves men's nature, their intrinsic design, vastly unnecessary. Led by one or two leaders, few men fulfill their God-given role in the church. The rest have no place.

In addition, there is no great battle. No assembling of armies for a combative surge. No team mission or exciting vision to conquer the competition. There's no need for strategizing, analyzing, and coaching an inspirational, against-all-odds victory. There's no championship to win. No pennant.

And that's plain wrong.

No wonder so many men stop coming. No wonder so many sit listless in the pews. Even non-Christian men, it is my assertion, are turned off because there is nothing connecting with their deep waters, what is truest about their hearts. Of course, that isn't the only reason. Paul says we are "the aroma of Christ among those who are being saved and those who are perishing. To the one we are the smell of death; to the other, the fragrance of life" (1 Cor. 2:15-16). But how alarming it would be if we are turning men away because they instinctively know what they are and see no place for it. Can we blame them for being uninterested?

The natural leaders, the men—those with a God-given nature to lead—have walked into a place where there were no opportunities to lead and quite naturally left. They may not have known why. Perhaps there was simply a lack of desire to return. And many never did.

Yet we wonder where the men have gone.

What may be worse, still, are those who never left. Perhaps through a trudging sense of duty, an unfulfilled desire to grow, or what we term "maturity," they've remained. Most likely, they've become accustomed to this new pattern of Christianity and have forgotten their nature altogether.

Yet we wonder why these men won't lead their families.

The problem, simply put, is they have been given the assignment of assistant managers when they wanted to be home run hitters and team captains. They've been relegated to couriers when they dreamed of being generals. They've been offered the job of receptionists when they were born to run the company.

In the church, they've been made submitters, adapters, and followers when all they wanted was to lead, take risks, and be in charge of something exciting that *matters*.

Something inside them hasn't been content to sit in pews, listen, and at times pass the tithe plate. Like the kids who wandered into our club, they wanted to be leaders and didn't care to be participants, whether they knew it or not.

They were designed with that nature. Really, all they wanted was to be men.

THE PASTOR GAP

But the current church structure is not only a problem for men. It's a problem for pastors, as well. Men suffer from not having a natural outlet for their God-given abilities. Unsurprisingly, pastors suffer from carrying the burden of leadership themselves.

The pastor gives the sermon every Sunday. He meets with staff. He visits members in the hospital. He performs weddings and funerals, organizes Bible studies, prayer gatherings, and potlucks, and if he is like most pastors, does a thousand other things. Some would say, "Well, that's like Moses in the Old Testament." That could not be further from the truth. Moses' father-in-law, who was not a Jew and whose faith is largely unknown, advised Moses to delegate his authority to capable men. Even Moses couldn't carry the Lord's people himself.

He saw it was right and did it.

If we understand this simple truth, it will change how we think about the church.

In the early church, there were twelve apostles and they appointed overseers (plural) in every local church. Deacons (again, plural), men with almost identical, rigorous qualifications, served under them. Whenever important tasks arose, the apostles appointed as many as they saw fit from a ready stable of capable men filled with the Holy Spirit. Think of Stephen and the six others who were chosen to wait on tables, all of whom were men "full of the Spirit and wisdom" (Acts 6:3).

Men took charge of roles of influence in the church and community. The first martyr, passionate about the mission, was killed fulfilling one. They were the New Testament equivalent of David's Mighty Men. Each powerfully persuaded the Word and ministered in the Holy Spirit. They were David's Thirty, who could each kill a tiger in a cave with a spear or single-handedly hold a field whilst his hand froze to the hilt of a sword.

Mighty men are products of such a church. Many were empowered in early church leadership.

Even the Old Testament picture of the church was a body whose duties, life, and leadership were built on the foundation of many strong men. Moses was the undisputed head, but the Levites, an entire twelfth of the Israelite men, including the high priest and his sons, served in a ministry even Moses wouldn't dare. And over the whole nation, he chose men as leaders "over thousands, hundreds, fifties, and tens" (Ex. 18:21). A portion of the Spirit was taken from Moses and put on the leaders to disperse the burden.

However, today, many pastors carry the burden alone. Even those with worship and youth pastors balance the weight of the church on the pastoral staff.

And an inherent separatism grows as pastors lead the church by themselves.

Few pastors feel they can have reciprocal relationships in their own churches because of this distance. I call it the pastor gap. It is the wide gulf between a pastor and his congregation in authority, responsibility, and regular life. This separation, which is a form of elitism, inevitably alienates him.

Community is a primary purpose of the church, but few pastors experience open and honest fellowship in their congregations. It is perhaps ironic. The same church that personifies love to the world is devoid of true friendship for many of its leaders.

The reason is simple. When such a huge burden of leadership is placed on a few men, or one man, a gap is created between them and the congregation. They are placed above it.

I have heard many say a higher conduct is required of pastors. That's not true. While the highest conduct is required of pastors (but not higher than other mature Christians), making it an elite position with extra-biblical rules and a standard of perfection creates the need for an *illusion* of higher conduct. This is perfectly accomplished by distance, the antithesis to fellowship. A pastor cannot appear to have problems because he is the One...and often he actually *is* the only one leading the congregation.

The Bible says he must be "above reproach" (1 Tim. 3:2). We have reinterpreted that as he should *appear* above reproach. So naturally, he must appear better than the rest. But this is in contrast to true holiness, which involves confession, brotherhood, and accountability. In addition to everything else on his desk, must he do this alone, too?

A pastor is just a man. If he is placed on a podium all alone, he will fall. Many pastors have.

The current structure of the church has elevated him to this place. The pastor of the modern-day church must be perfect. Since he is not, he must remain far enough out of touch from the congregants' lives for them to see it. This seems ridiculous, but there is more than a speck of saw dust worth of truth to this. There is perhaps an entire log.

In many ways, this is Christians' fault.

We set pastors up on a podium of perfection from which they cannot but topple. Sometimes our expectations extend beyond impossible to just plain weird. Let me give an example. A woman I know drove by her pastor's house while he was washing his car. He happened to have his shirt off (his Sunday best might not be appropriate for the spray-to-the-sky-and-try-to-drink-the-rain trick on a hot Florida day). She was so shocked she immediately left the church, claiming she could never look at him the same again.

It is silly to explain a pastor can wear the same board shorts when washing his car that he would at the beach. And honestly, I don't know too many topless pastors who would inspire unholy thoughts when getting sudsy. But if one has dirt or scratches in his life deeper than those on his Dodge Ram, is not the church the family to whom he is supposed to turn? Are not the brothers of this family the ones who should clean him?

So the very entity meant to be his support system, his lifeline—the church—becomes his deathtrap.

Imagine the isolation living in the community Jesus prayed would be one as God is One, God's crowd of love, acceptance, and brotherhood, and finding oneself alone.

Inevitably, accountability also suffers. I believe many pastors have fallen into grievous sin because they lacked open, heartfelt accountability with members in their own body. Far more common, I imagine, are those who don't struggle with major sin, but groan inwardly for a "friend who sticks closer than a brother" (Prov. 18:24) with whom to share the joys of life.

Oh, I know, they go outside the local body to other pastors. *Only pastors can understand other pastors' problems.* But that is simply not true. God has given a measure of wisdom to all. More importantly, they are brothers. Isn't it logical the members of a local body should care for their own, even their pastor?

More poignantly, if a pastor doesn't have mature men in his church with whom he can openly and honestly share life, that is the most telling indication of the state of his church. No matter how large it may be, it is a dying and stagnant church if no other men stand with him. And the church will remain stagnant if it isn't turning men other than the pastor into leaders.

Something is indeed wrong with the current church, and at its core, I believe it's a misconception of who the pastor is meant to be in relation to the other men. Of course, the pastor has authority in the church. God desires we hold him in high respect. But I don't think God ever intended the gap that exists between pastors and other men, today. One has to admit something is certainly missing. For starters, let's say—*all the other men.*

And that hints at what this book is about. Every man is meant to be empowered, to lead, to live out his nature as God intended. It's a nature—if we understand it—that will change the church.

This book embarks upon a journey to reveal the beauty of *who* we are, but just as importantly, *how* God desires the church to change. Draw close to him. Listen along the way. If you do, I'm convinced you'll catch a vision of the simple, unmistakable call on the heart of every man and on Christ's Bride, the church.

Yet, it really is simple.

There are steps to help each man become a leader. In church, we muddy the topic with words like "discipleship" that mean the steps to help him become the leader he's meant to be. But make no mistake; it is the destiny of every man to become one. God has written it on his heart.

And that should be the goal of every pastor. To help him read it there.

-Chapter Two-
MASCULINITY

If he says that one more time, I'm going over there.

It was my junior year of high school. I was lounging in the back of Spanish I, while a sub covered for our teacher who was sick. Or had found something better to do than give 25 kids a verb conjugation quiz.

The sub, like most I remember from high school, quickly fulfilled her one assignment of losing control of the class.

On this particular day, however, the students were surprisingly quiet. Only one student spoke—an upperclassman who was repeatedly yelling at a freshman girl the sex act she had supposedly done with him at a party that weekend.

Expletives and all.

The sub stopped her lesson, stood back, and *did nothing*.

In the grand scheme of things, there are only so many times a guy can listen to, "Didn't you [insert rude phrase here]," shouted at the top of another guy's lungs.

Looking back, I see what happened in a blur. There really was no choice what to do. For a godly man, there rarely is.

So it came to be, on an ordinary autumn school day, relaxing in the back of the class in an 80's metal Anthrax T-shirt (it was 1997) and black combat boots, I made my first silent ultimatum in a classroom.

As I listened to my fellow upperclassman thoroughly humiliate the little freshman, my fists clenched harder and harder.

If he says that one more time...

I was reaching a breaking point. And when I reach breaking points, things happen.

I turned to the two guys next to me and slowly uttered, "If he says that one more time, I'm going over there."

Their eyes widened. Something in my face told them I was serious.

One whispered, "He benches 250 (lbs)."

I glared back. The words popped out.

"I bench 255."

A certain not-so-friendly classmate shouted another predictably not-so-friendly phrase. One more time.

And I rose to my feet.

Staring straight ahead with Terminator focus, I marched (strutted might be appropriate) around the classroom and stopped over his seat.

My chest in his face.

I glared at him. "I don't appreciate the way you're treating her. I want you to apologize right now."

His eyes raced every direction.

"Who is this guy?!? Who is this? Who's this guy in front of me?

The only place he didn't look was at me.

My tone was steel. "I said, 'I want you to apologize, *right now.*'"

I'll never understand this, but it was at this moment the sub broke out of her trance at the front of the room and made her one contribution to the class telling *me* to go sit down.

A moment later, I returned to my seat.

And that guy didn't say *a word* the rest of class.

Although I didn't realize it at the time, Anthrax shirt, combat boots, bad fashion, and all, who I was as a man was being formed every time I stood up.

WHERE WE ARE NOW

We often have a different view of godly masculinity. If we recognize it, at all.

I read an article today that said the words masculinity and femininity aren't in the Bible. They are simply humanistic ideas. The author went on to make a superficial argument that all Christians are just people following Christ, with the only relevant distinction being the cross, man or woman. This viewpoint of interchangeable roles is very popular to a secular society. Since the feminist movement of the 1970s, it has gained popularity among Christians, as well. Even those who believe there are differences between men and women rarely extend them past a few roles or a few generalities.

We concede women sighing over babies, attending toe painting parties, and sharing juicy tidbits about relationships. We nod and smirk at men picking up blunted objects and creating games that leave echoes of raucous laughter and a few scars. I suppose a few of us roll our eyes and shake our heads in surrender. We know that boys will be boys but should someday learn to be men who hold doors for ladies. We recognize that chairs pulled in deference show a certain pause of strength in the presence of beauty. We may say this strength is a fortress for that beauty, to which it entrusts its life and security. And the wonder of it all, at the heart of this are a woman's compassion and capacity for love that marvel even creation as it holds its breath.

But is there really more? Can such beauty actually be biblical in the face of a skeptical pop culture? In the face of a crumbling church worldview?

To find out, one must start at the beginning.

Elisabeth Elliot, famed writer of *Passion and Purity* and *Let Me Be a Woman,* wrote another, slightly less prolific book called *The Mark of a Man*. Along with a tool belt and a Bible concordance, in the presence of a small group of men I respected, my dad gave me this book on my 21st birthday. My brothers and I often remark that we consider it the definitive book on being a man. Interestingly, it's written by a woman. I suppose she should know.

In it, Elliot outlines the beginning, man and God, and God presenting a breathtaking new creation to man—woman. She notes four important details in that story: 1) Eve is made for the man, 2) She is made from the man, 3) She is brought to the man, and 4) She is named by the man. This is the account of the beginning. He is in no way better. In fact, she may be God's perfect finishing touch. But there are certainly hints at differences in those first pages of history.

Before we look at Scripture further, it's important to make a point. As Americans in the 21st century, we don't like being told what to do. We don't like rules. We push five to seven over the speed limit, just enough to hope not to get a ticket. The more reckless of us zoom past construction zones to the chagrin of orange-clad laborers. We certainly don't like being given roles, either. When we feel typecast, we complain the norm can't represent us and our whole focus becomes breaking it. Naturally, when we feel oppressed by a rule we don't understand, we buck it.

From working with students, I know this only too well. I've found high-schoolers don't respond enthusiastically to "because I said so." Neither do we in the church. Unfortunately, however, "because God said so" has been the pat line for the church's teaching on gender roles for decades.

And that misses the point. The reason God says so is because *it matters*. Like high-schoolers, as men and women we need to know why before we can fully embrace God's roles for us. We've made ourselves a need-to-know culture, and it's probably time we knew.

After all, we can't fully be what God calls us to be without first knowing what that is. Sadly, many churches don't teach it, and many have practices that don't line up with who God says we are because they don't fully understand it.

The problem begins with the paradigm. We're so focused on roles we miss what God is focused on: *design*. He has a purpose that drives his plan. And there is a nature one will never take out of any man. Or any woman. That's not just the nature of Christ. Our life in Christ doesn't replace the natures of a man and woman God gave us *from the beginning.* Rather, it augments them, perfecting us in who God originally intended us to be.

And God's word clearly points to what that is. He shows us in His design.

A MASCULINE GOD

Father of creation, he rules on high. "Heaven is [his] throne and the earth is [his] footstool" (Is. 66:1). There is something fierce about the nature of God. He is vehemently jealous for his Bride, so much so that he endures centuries of heartache, longing, anger, breakup, daring rescue, sacrifice, battle, death, and resurrection for her.

He obliterates enemies that challenge her. With a swipe of his hand, he destroys all who dare oppose her. He fathers her, guides and disciples her, dies for her, but lets her decide to follow. Not domineering or oppressive, he leads her, but allows her to walk away. He allows her to choose. She has a response; that is her responsibility.

The design starts with God. Mess with the design and you mess with the nature of God. You mess with who he is. That's why it bothers me so much when churches teach contrary to God's word on gender issues, when they eliminate masculinity and femininity for a more palatable gospel, whether in the family or the church. They don't understand and are therefore distorting *him.*

We know men and women are made in the image of God. "Male and female he created them" (Gen. 1:27). So as to get the distinction, it repeats later in Genesis 5:2, "He created them male and female and blessed them."

Why he, first of all? Why not the Grand It?

I mean, really, The I Am would be a perfectly neutral, acceptable reference to God. It even sounds cool. But the coolness factor is not a gauge God uses in determining his nature. Quite truly, he is who he is, and it's not going to change for our whim. Gender-neutralizing God would destroy his character, which is inherently masculine in relation to us. And that has *meaning*.

But what is masculinity? If you know God, then you already know. Masculinity is authority, leadership, protection, provision, and strength. He cares for us, watches over us, teaches and leads us. He is strong, mighty to save us. And we can trust him.

Although it may sound shocking, the relationship of a husband to a wife is the same. Ephesians says, "The husband is the head of the wife, as Christ is the head of the church" (5:23). And later, when describing a man's relationship to his wife, "This mystery is great; but I am speaking with reference to Christ and the church" (5:32, NASB). But he is also speaking about a man and his wife, which shows the parallel perfectly.

The comparison teaches us so much about God.

The mystery is Christ taking a husband's role to his Bride. He uses husbands and wives to show his nature. The complexity is lost if we drop the analogy. And so is the beauty.

In case we haven't picked it up, we are the Bride. For to us, God is masculine. He is a "refuge...a stronghold in time of trouble (Psalm 9:9)," he "rescue[s] the poor...the needy from those who rob them" (Psalm 35:10), and he "guides [us] in paths of righteousness for his name's sake" (Psalm 23:3).

Protects, rescues, teaches, leads. Masculine qualities that originate in strength.

We can't miss God's relationship to us. His Word tells us to look in a man's relationship to his wife.

They are tied up in relationship together. We learn so much about each through the analogy—God's analogy. It almost sounds blasphemous to a progressive pop culture, but it is exactly God's Word.

1 Corinthians 11:3 says, "But I want you to realize that Christ is the head of every man, and the man is the head of a woman, and God is the head of Christ" (NASB).

The connection is so simple. To deny it is to deny God.

MASCULINITY: THE EVIDENCE

If men have this nature of masculinity, the design should match the command. And it does.

Men are protectors, strong. They lead and guide their wives. They provide security; the same nature of masculinity as God. That's why Boaz became Ruth's kinsman-*redeemer*. It's why men are called to be the savior of the body for their wives "as Christ is [for] the church" (Eph. 5:23). And it's why loving a wife as Christ loved the church looks like being willing to die for her or live for her in a daily, practical way.

We see a man's strength is physical, whether Samson or a carpenter's son, but also emotional, with the level-headedness of Solomon, who leads a kingdom, or Jacob, who maneuvers a family. Men's logic and reasoning may infuriate a woman in the heat of emotion, but can save a family or church in time of direction. The definitive characteristic is strength, whether physical or emotional. This kind of strength would allow David to survive for years in caves, focusing on God's promise of the kingdom. It will enable men, today, to navigate their families through joblessness, depression, or fear.

It is in a godly man's nature to be strong and with it to protect, lead, guide.

My dad was this leader to me. Whatever I did, he made his specialty—studying it, mastering it, and helping me do the same. He wrestled for the University of Michigan, so when I joined my high school team, he frequented the room, wrestling with all the guys.

Masculinity

Those days were fresh and surreal, filled with indelible memories. I remember one practice the entire team stopped as he battled a match against our captain, an upperclassman we revered. It was a close 4-3 score, and I don't remember to this day who won.

A particular memory comes back from that time. Our team was competing in a six team tournament in Novi, Michigan. Dad was along as a volunteer, but one who'd earned the respect of the team. We found ourselves in a competitive meet, and it would come down to the final match.

Our 215 pounder was battling fiercely with his opponent when he was injured by an illegal move. Josh, I'll call him, was a sincere, friendly guy, one who wouldn't harm a fly if it wasn't wearing a singlet. An honest kid, he would finish the match if possible. When Dad and the coaches got him back to the corner it became clear; he couldn't continue. Josh would win on illegal injury default.

The opposing team's coach, a hulking man who moonlit as a bar bouncer, lumbered over and began spitting insults at Josh, accusing him of faking the injury to win. Dad jumped up and charged at him, meeting him half-way between the benches. He stuck his chest out, his arms pulled back behind him like the wings of a swan threatened in the wild, his chin jutting up at him. He fired back, challenging the coach to a match right there.

It would help to mention my dad is 5'7 and fifteen years ago weighed ten pounds *less* than the 152 he weighs now. Quite a contrast to the behemoth before him.

I will never forget the image of my dad's fierceness, standing down the giant over a boy with questions in his eyes.

Jesus raging against the money-changers in the temple, turning over tables, and driving them back with a whip.

These things a boy does not quickly forget. They're things that shape him. The moment is impressed upon my memory. It is a defining one. It is a picture of a man's strength.

Last year, I received a card from Cinque Carter, the wrestler on that team with whom I became eventual co-captain. It was with a gift he sent for my wedding. What caught my eye was the way it was signed: the black Demsick brother. Fifteen years after any significant connection between us, he nearly flew 1,300 miles to the wedding. And when I spoke to him, the first words out of his mouth were, as usual, "How's your dad?"

He communicated everything to me in that question.

I know what my dad was to him—the same he was to me. The black Demsick brother, my brother, son of the same man.

The wrestlers on that team acted differently around my dad. They didn't swear or pick on each other when he was around. He never asked them not to. But they recognized him as a man to be respected. A man of strength. The integrity he brought to that team left its impression on the boys who admired him years after his physical presence in their lives had gone.

And it remains still. I hear it in the lingering tone of a question.

THE COUNTERFEIT

The world, in contrast, uses strength to benefit itself. To the victor go the spoils. The survival of the fittest. Worldly strength is the counterfeit of godly strength.

I suppose it's no surprise some men use power for selfishness. There's no end to the brutality of strength gone bad. Rape, murder, molestation, and domestic violence are all predominantly male crimes. In the home, a man may not use his fists, but his strength as intimidation strikes as deadly a blow with no bruise. Even a man who bulldozes his wife, "lording it over her," uses strength for evil. He isn't a man. He is a bully.

Angela and I were discussing recently how lucky we were our fathers saw their job as one of sacrifice to our families. If the

Demsick Friday night movie was my mom's favorite screwball comedy, *My Man, Godfrey,* or a western like *The Magnificent Seven*, we were watching the world's wittiest butler. Unless the boys were in a shooting mood (which we often were). And the Bar None candy bars were cowboy rations or servants' pay the four of us gobbled up. Dad never used his position for himself. He put Mom and the boys first. His luxury was to love.

Any guy who uses strength or position for his own comfort needs to reassess why he was given leadership. He must instantly humble himself before God, seek him, and allow God to show him how to serve.

But, perhaps less noticeably, pride can creep into a guy's heart. It's surprising how little we may be involved in a sport or area of study before we think we own the topic. *We are the experts*. If we aren't paying attention, careful to remain humble, it will corrode our childlike response to God.

Jesus said, "I tell you the truth, anyone who will not receive the kingdom of God like a little child will not enter it" (Mark 10:15). God values childlike humility and faith in him. No matter how big our biceps.

There's something satisfying in my soul when I cultivate a subordinate attitude in church, a Bible study, or a meeting rather than criticize or imagine I could do it better. It feels good to remember I'm still a child before God. Still able to learn.

THE COWARD

But perhaps I'm in the minority. I don't believe a man must be weak to be used by God. God desires that a man is confident in his *strength*. I'm not one to tell people to be weak so God can be strong. God wants men to know they are strong, without a hint of question in their core. David was such a man. He was fiercely confident he could take out lions or bears. And he had no doubt of his abilities against giants.

But he *trusted* God, not his strength. Confidence in his strength, trust in God, the source of strength and victory. These two can co-exist.

God isn't aiming for weakness. He wants to hone our strength as David did against animals in the wild. God relishes making you strong as a father would a son. But he wants you to remain humble and grateful to him in the process.

I suppose this is where the other extreme of masculinity comes in. If it isn't the counterfeit, roaring as a pretense of strength but doing no good, it's the coward who is unaware of his strength and incapable of using it.

God wants men to stand up. To know they are strong. And it's time they do.

THE MIGHTY MEN

There's a group of heroes in the Old Testament who exemplify this. They are David's Mighty Men. I believe the Mighty Men are symbols of a deeper strength of masculinity God created in every man.

Those who cower from challenges or shirk leadership responsibilities, waiting for their wives or women in their churches to pick up the slack, need to realize God made each of them a Mighty Man.

Every man is meant to cut down armies.

If a man finds insecurity creeping into his heart, he must go to God for his identity, to the Mighty Man verses and those that speak of his valiant nature. Perhaps time with brothers bow hunting in deep woods, shooting at the range, catching waves off the coast, or camping in a state park will remind him. Heck, standing on the kitchen countertop singing rousing songs at the top of his lungs.

It doesn't matter, so long as there's a twinge of risk or adventure—a fierceness one man reflects in another. That's how brothers call to brothers' deep hearts. "As iron sharpens iron," the proverb says (Prov. 27:17).

But, no matter how he feels, one thing every man must do. He must play the man.

In 2 Samuel 10:12, the Israelite army is surrounded and outnumbered. The odds are against them and they know it. But God and his people have been offended. They will fight. In what I imagine is an epically inspiring moment, Joab addresses his troops. He rallies his warriors with these words: "Be strong and let us fight bravely for our people and the cities of our God. The Lord will do what is good in his sight."

The King James Version translates "let us fight bravely" an interesting way. It says, "let us play the man for our people and for the cities of our God."

These men are daunted by approaching armies. They'd probably rather shear sheep right now than be heroes. But Joab holds them to the task, reminding them to "play the man." Whether they feel like it or not, this is their time. They must be strong and play the part God has given them as brave warriors. God's people depend on it.

My dad loved to tell me and my brothers this story growing up.

For that is what a man must do. If he is filled with fear, it's time to strap on his boots, be strong, and play the man. It's the part God has prepared for him. There is no substitute for taking on a manly attitude, wrapping one's fingers around the hilt of a sword, and going to war.

Shearing sheep is no alternative on this battlefield.

For God has made us strong. It is the defining fiber of our being. We've been created with it in our blueprint. Like a hero reborn through some freak genetic government project, strength is a code God engineered within the framework of our DNA. We have a destiny we cannot reject. We were born for it. The time will come in our story when we realize it, and then...watch out. I'd hate to be an opposing army then. Even against one man.

One Mighty Man.

STRENGTH FOR BEAUTY

In a symbolic way, that's why men open doors for ladies. In a practical way, it's why they jump out of helicopters in rocky terrains and chase down nightmares. They conquer evil, fighting like their Father to protect the family and people they love.

Just the very presence of masculine strength puts a woman at ease. There's a special way it quiets her heart. It says nothing will touch you tonight.

This isn't true because God merely says men are leaders, protectors, and providers. It's in the nature of things. He proves it. He resonates through every fiber of creation the same resounding message. The beauty is in the differences. This is the "great mystery."

Christ and the church. Man and woman. Strength and beauty.

Two completely different natures. Two totally different purposes. If you don't understand yours, you'll never live it out, never know how to play your part. You may find yourself yearning for another role, not recognizing the one you *were born to play.*

Amazingly, God ordained it this way. It really shouldn't surprise us, though; the hints are everywhere. When we choose not to see them, we jumble everything up. But if we look closer, we'll learn so much about who we were created to be. And we'll see, too, it is very good.

In the next chapter, we'll take a closer look at man's nature and, more specifically, at God's Word. The wonder of His plan will come to light in what we find reflected there.

It will become awesome as we unveil it.

-*Chapter Three*-
A BOY'S BATTLES

It was the week before the fourth football game of my brother Rob's senior year.

"We're not leaving this field until the offense gains five yards!"

Rob perked up. In that moment, he decided, *We're not going home.*

A transfer from a local school, he was lauded as an elite wrestler, but joined the football team, as well, to try his skills at another sport.

However, the way his new team practiced, quite frankly, disgusted him. A quarter through the season, it was time to show them why football is considered a contact sport.

And he'd been learning.

He'd learned he could watch the linemen's feet and predict which way a run was developing. That was a unique skill on the scout team defense, which meant the scraps left over after the starting offensive and defensive squads were assembled.

As usual, the coach wanted to see the offense churn out some yards against the garbage time defense before sending everyone home. But a wrestler who's tired of watching guys a hundred pounds more than him sandbag through practice can take that as some sort of challenge.

And he'd had enough of the imitation of toughness.

Rob was a linebacker; he liked hitting. He had a philosophy in those days, one that has since become a Demsick philosophy. He accepted that contact hurts. He was okay with it. So he decided he'd *bring the pain* and try to make it hurt as much as possible. He found whenever he followed that philosophy, it would hurt like crazy and the other person would fall down.

For a future physics professor, it was a discovery of impressive higher-level thought.

After a few hits from Rob, the linemen on his team tiptoed more delicately when he was their blocking assignment.

On this particular day, he was fed up with the lack of effort by a team more interested in the Friday night after-party than winning, more concerned about which cheerleaders they were dating than the blood, sweat, and guts of a hard-fought victory.

And he realized, in that moment, he could single-handedly teach them a lesson.

We're not leaving this field.

The first play swept to his side. He jammed the lead blocker, backed him into the running back, and slammed him to the ground for a loss.

Feet to the right, he noticed.

The next play developed to the other side of the field. He darted over, knifed through, and rocked the stunned running back. The other linebacker's assignment. No gain.

The ball carrier rumbled his way again. Rob stuffed the line—crunching body parts in his 170 pound frame against 225, 240 pound walls of increasingly timid linemen. And pounced on the running back.

Sliced through the other side for a diving tackle.

Pounded the lead blocker and halfback on his side.

Whichever way the ball went, Rob raced to make the tackle.

Pacing back and forth on the sideline, the head coach fumed, straining to figure out why his beloved offense was falling apart. Amidst personal attacks on the character of the offensive linemen, he barked the threat, "We're not leaving this field until the offense gains five yards!"

Then he turned to Rob and winked.

After four or five more bone-jarring hits, no matter which way the ball went, and not an inch budged, the coach sheepishly blew the whistle.

"Alright, that's enough for the day," he mumbled and began to jog in. They never gained the five yards.

In twelve plays, not another player on the defense made a single tackle.

The head coach shuffled over to his defensive coordinator and grunted, "Demsick!"

Rob ran over.

Putting his arm around the defensive coordinator's shoulder and leaning in, without even glancing at Rob, he said dryly, "How 'bout starting *Demsick* at linebacker Friday."

The coordinator got the hint. Rob started the rest of the season and averaged eleven tackles a game.

A MAN'S NATURE

Men are certainly unique. Women laugh about men stubbornly refusing to ask for directions. They shrug their shoulders at the thought of us tramping around in the mud, covered in camouflage, hoping to rain down skin-piercing paint pellets on our best friends before they rain on us. Perhaps there is something strange to that. But I don't see it. The grain of my programming goes so deep, there was no first lesson and no drill, and there will be no final exam. There's no questioning it. I'm not the product of my baby room color. Don't even know what that was.

My programming goes back to the beginning of time when God created the world. His directions came long after. Why haven't we looked deeper to find the natures of man and woman?

So many Christians and churches in our society considerably contort themselves to sidestep God's clear directions to men and women. Perhaps they wouldn't struggle so hard if they stepped back and looked at what God created, at the differences between them. His creation was so beautiful from the beginning.

And a good place to begin is with boys. Apparently, they say, "boys will be boys." Do they? Do they really admit there is something different about them?

"If they do, it's probably weirdness," I can practically hear my wife say. She may be right. But if there's something unique about being a boy and we recognize it, then it makes sense there's something unique about being a man, as well.

The clues in young boyhood should be pretty indicative of what that uniqueness is. Just as DNA scripts were written at conception and God's patterns were written alongside time, so the nature of man was written long before he decided whether he would be an astronaut or police officer, long before he dreamt of his first kiss.

Imaginary superheroes and monsters, six shooters and bazookas, secret missions and legendary last stands.

This is a boy's world, his theater. He takes his place on this stage of humanity to play a part.

But the script was written long before.

A BOY'S BATTLES

When I was little I used to play with G.I. Joes. My three brothers—Robert, Doy, and Richard—and I would enact epic battles that lasted for hours. More than a few G.I. Joes lie buried in anonymous grave sites on hallowed grounds where we once played. Those places remain sacred in my mind even now. A little boy's battles leave an immeasurable imprint on him. In memory, they are larger than life. They prepare him for a much larger life and much truer battles.

One of the battles of a man's soul is to maintain that sense of wonder. If he never loses belief in what was truest about him when he was a boy, he will be a strong man indeed. If along the way he believes he is incapable there, his strength will be crippled as a man. Childhood is a fantastical, imaginary time for a boy, but it is also training grounds for becoming a man. And it indicates most clearly what a man is.

I remember one of the games I used to play with Robert, who was closest in age to me: Lego battles. Really, it was just Legos, but it always ended with a battle. Four hours of building armies, scenes, and back-stories and fifteen minutes of destroying them was the norm on a Saturday for the two of us. We'd spill out the contents of our enormous bins on Looney Tunes blankets and begin the day's adventure.

One scene we particularly liked was woodsmen and knights. I had one I ingeniously named Speary who, you guessed it, held a spear in each hand. He was my champion, my finest warrior. Not to be outdone, my slightly younger, but just as crafty, brother had a woodsman he named Axey. Axey, brilliantly, held an axe.

More than a few funny altercations I see from those days when I look back. Me playing the older brother act and working in lines of dialogue (Yes, there was dialogue) about how Speary was so much better than Axey. Come to think of it, I think my worst guy was better than Axey.

Of course, Robert would have nothing to do with it. Axey, he claimed, was every bit the elite warrior as Speary, and I'm sure on good days, he was better. Still, I remember waddling my saddest duck of a woodsman over to him, the one with the pirate's eye patch and no hand, and casually saying to Axey, "It's okay. I'm stupid too."

I wonder if that's a scene many girls would be caught acting out. Axey and Speary. Competing for who is the best fighter and who's just stupid too.

My wife used to watch her sister play with dolls. I hear her stories were quite elaborate, as well. I wonder how many people died. I'm guessing Speary would've died from heartbreak or a freak shopping accident, or at his unluckiest, after a long life, congestive heart failure. But I bet he would've made an amazing prince.

And that's what I'm getting at.

God's design is awesome if we take it in. It might surprise us how intricate and complex it is, probably far more so than we've imagined. The differences and how perfectly they fit together, if we understood them fully, would astound us. They'd take our breath away.

But we don't have to take it on blind faith. All we have to do is open our eyes once in a while.

And when it comes to God's Word, we have to listen.

THE SCRIPT: GOD'S WORD

In the beginning of Genesis, God presents Eve to Adam. She is not his possession, but his responsibility. These details about the beginning *matter*.

Adam is created with strength and authority. Eve is created as the complement to him, a "help-meet" with an opposite nature that exactly fits. Together they are the perfect pair. He is designed to lead, she to follow. He is designed with authority, she with nurturing and support. He with strength, she with beauty. She is much more than that, but that is a starting point.

For man, evidence is everywhere that his design matches this role, in the nature of boys at play and the nature of men at war. From young men who crowd around board games for hours of strategy, espionage, and diplomacy, to men like the Proverbs 31 woman's husband who "sits among the elders of the land" (Prov. 31:23) discussing theological matters and justice. In each, a similar thread of masculinity emerges as one observes creation.

Battle. Strategy. Authority. Power. In a word, testosterone. Of course, it is exactly for these God biologically engineered men with testosterone. This, too, shows a purpose.

But men's nature isn't only evident in life; it is clearly indicated in God's Word.

Romans 5:19 says, "For just as through the disobedience of the one man the many were made sinners, so also through the obedience of the one man the many will be made righteous."

Jesus is the one who made all righteous. That is clarified in the chapter.

Adam, not Eve, is the one who caused the world's disobedience. The first Adam. It is repeated throughout the verses. The second would come to change all that.

Adam was given the responsibility to lead and protect. When he gave up his role, forgetting his initiative to look out for Eve's welfare (as well as all creation's), disobedience began.

What we need to not miss is that the burden of responsibility on man from the beginning was because Adam was *designed* to lead and protect. He was made with a totally different physiological and spiritual nature than Eve. This genetic make-up, from the beginning, was very good.

And if we understand it, it will redefine how we think about men and women in the family and church today.

Consider Gideon, Joshua, David, Samson, Moses, Jacob; the list goes on and on. Godly men who displayed their faith by charging into battles with trumpets and torches, scouting territories, killing giants and leading renegade bands of warriors, mauling armies, confronting kings and leading a nation, strategizing a legacy and wrestling a god.

Countless masculine examples displaying the qualities of godly masculinity.

But God doesn't only show us examples of men who exhibit the power and authority of biblical manhood in his Word. He doesn't simply make what may be known about God "plain to [us], because God has made it plain…" (Rom. 1:19).

He tells us.

UNCOVERING DESIGN

God gives direct instructions to back it up.

"The head of the woman is man" (1 Cor. 11:3).

The verses that follow are some of the least taught in the Bible. That's probably because no one follows them literally. Their exact application in today's society is not my focus here, what they're saying about men and women is.

Immediately after saying "the head of the woman is man," Paul writes:

> Every man who has something on his head while praying or prophesying disgraces his head. But every woman who has her head uncovered while praying or prophesying disgraces her head, for she is one and the same as the woman whose head is shaved. For if a woman does not cover her head, let her also have her hair cut off; but if it is disgraceful for a woman to have her hair cut off or her head shaved, let her cover her head.

> For a man ought not to have his head covered, since he is the image and glory of God; but the woman is the glory of man. For man does not originate from woman, but woman from man; for indeed man was not created for the woman's sake, but woman for the man's sake. Therefore the woman ought to have *a symbol of authority* on her head, because of the angels. However, in the Lord, neither is woman independent of man, nor is man independent of woman. For as the woman originates from the man, so also the man has his birth through the woman; and all things originate from God.

> Judge for yourselves: is it proper for a woman to pray to God with her head uncovered? Does not even nature itself teach you that if a man has long hair, it is a dishonor to him, but if a woman has long hair, it is a glory to her? For her hair is given to her for a covering. But if one is inclined to be contentious, we have no other practice, nor have the churches of God. (NASB, emphasis mine)

We have a culture far removed from women wearing head pieces in church. Many Christians think that makes the passage irrelevant or only written for a certain time period. But no Bible verse is irrelevant. Every one is saying something crucial about God and something about us. Read the passage closer and it cannot possibly be; it reveals God's nature, as well as ours.

Paul says it's so important for women to display men's authority that they wear head pieces (probably shawls) when believers gather together. Now, I don't remember the last time I've seen shawls in church. Or even hoodies, for that matter. But this passage is certainly not about a legalistic requirement for women to wear shawls. It is about the *nature* of men and women.

Paul is trying to make a point. He wants it to stick and for us to back it up with action. Notice how he refers to nature and long hair? He is getting at original design. There is a plan and two very different, inherent natures. That's what this passage is about.

In it, Paul says woman should wear head pieces as *a symbol of authority*. The authority he means is no mystery, it starts the passage—that man is the head of woman. And the symbol has meaning. One always does.

It points to design.

Men were created to lead. That's their nature.

Women should display their relationship to men, one of following, in church. That's why most passages that talk about men and women in church have some element of submission or quietness on the part of women included. It's not to keep them down. It's to help us see how he created our relationships to work. The more we live it out, the healthier we will be.

That's God's way, not man's. It's simply nature.

He's the one who designed us. It's interesting these directions are not only for our benefit, though, but "because of the angels." Could it be they would be offended if we did not tangibly observe the differences?

However, to keep men in check, Paul mitigates this powerful statement about authority by saying, "Hey, but don't forget, men, you aren't independent of her; she births you." In other words, don't get cocky with that leadership.

The really striking part is how Paul finishes. This is where the progressive, liberal culture and the church succumbing to its Sirens should take note. After an entire passage indicating God's clear design, Paul finishes with: "*But if one is inclined to be contentious, we have no other practice, nor have the churches of God.*"

Whoa.

Don't pick a fight with God.

Sounds a lot like Revelation 22:18-19. "I testify to everyone who hears the words of the prophecy of this book: if anyone adds to them, God will add to him the plagues...in this book. And if anyone takes away from the words of the book of this prophecy, God will take away his part from the tree of life and from the holy city...."

God throws down the gauntlet on anyone who messes with his Word. So does Paul. There's no room to remove masculinity from men, or its purpose from the home or church.

We have seen the hints of it. The evidence is in men and boys, as clear as anything in God's creation. And He has said it plainly. He's added, "Back off; don't mess with it. This is the way it's done in God's church everywhere." And it's the way it should be done today. Because once again, if we reject God's instructions, we're only rejecting God.

That one little phrase, "because of the angels," is God's clue. He's saying important spiritual matters are represented in these practices. They are symbols for huge spiritual realities. Rejecting them offends the angels. Throughout the Old Testament, angels are synonymous with the Lord. Rejecting masculinity and femininity—who we are at our essence—offends him.

The point I'm making isn't to argue women must wear head pieces in church. It's that the natures of men and women they indicate are crucial. It's to argue who we are.

That is Paul's point. The visible display of male leadership in the church is important enough to Paul to make an issue of it. Do you see here that who we are as men and women is intrinsically different in ways that matter? At its most basic level, the passage shows this topic of men's and women's design goes a lot deeper than we realize. And God is in the middle of it.

INSIDE THE MYSTERY

But God gets more specific in his directions for authority. He tells men they are the "head of the wife as Christ is the head of the church" (Eph. 5:23).

God has placed men in charge, just as Christ is to them.

And isn't that the appropriate use of strength?

Unsurprisingly, this fits perfectly with 1 Corinthians saying "the head of every man is Christ, the head of the woman is man, and the head of Christ is God." These are all powerfully analogous relationships, and we're meant to learn from their comparisons.

We are, in fact, in a very profound way, the image of God.

It would be blasphemous to say men have a different relationship to women than Christ does to the church. God has said the opposite. The term head becomes clear with this analogy. We are a body. Life does not merely originate with the head; the head instructs it. Similarly, Christ is the One who directs.

Displaying the awe of this relationship, man is analogous to God. That's why man is "the glory of God," while woman is "the glory of man" (1 Cor. 11:7). Both are the image of God and equal. But in the relationship, one represents God, the other represents man. This is what is held in the awe of the mystery of Christ and the church. Dare we mess it up?

Rather, we should dig deeper to fully understand it.

At heart, a man is characterized by strength, authority, protection, and provision. He is a leader.

It is who God made him to be.

If a woman tries to imitate or rival him, she weakens him and hinders herself. If he relinquishes his role, whether by misunderstanding or passivity, they are both hurt and the deep waters of his heart, clouded. But God created them to be drawn out, and a man of understanding will find them.

These deep waters hold the mystery of his heart. If one stares into them long enough, one will see mirrored a strong, godly man, unique and noble, awesome and intimidating, everything God designed him to be. No one can rival him. No one can replace him.

The same is true of her.

-Chapter Four-
FEMININITY

When I first saw it in a gallery in L.A., I knew I had to have it.

The painting, now my favorite, is titled, "Gargoyles," by Michael Parkes. It depicts a young girl, likely coming of age as a woman, who stands atop a stone ledge facing out at blue sky that surrounds her. Beside her lie a teddy bear and jump rope, which appear haphazardly tossed aside. Before her, she blows bubbles from a little wand that drift off the building and across the painting's expansive sky.

What are unique are the gargoyles perched atop the building. Each has come to life. One snarls, roaring in disbelief at the bubbles. Another, most strikingly, jumps off the rooftop, holding a hand over its heart, a look of sheer determination on its face. Its other hand reaches out for the farthest bubble.

The moment I stumbled upon it, ambling through little niche shops and trendy galleries, I instantly recognized in it a picture of masculinity and femininity, complex, yet breathtakingly beautiful. The girl is becoming a woman and blows her bubbles—her deepest dreams and desires—off the rooftop of her heart and into the blue sky of wonder and possibility. I saw in the gargoyles the stereotypical, cold-hearted male. She catches the attention of one, which roars but does nothing—a superficial version of masculinity. He is all noise and no action.

The other is so mesmerized by her beauty and, more importantly, the beauty of her heart that he comes to life. The bubbles, her dreams, float before him. Roused to life, he breaks from his mold of stone, which crumbles beneath his feet, and leaps.

The gargoyle has no concern for the ledge or the fall beneath him. Only the girl's dreams that blow carelessly off the rooftop before him matter. He is so inspired that he reaches for the farthest one. The look of determination on his face shows he lives in this leap far more than he ever did on the ledge.

That is what a woman can do to a man.

It is how a true man encounters beauty and is changed by it. He does not roar and remain on the ledge.

He leaps.

He does not consider the fall. He is too enchanted by her dreams.

Perhaps more than my words can, the picture of this painting captures what is so profound about a woman's heart. It captures her tender, sensitive beauty. It captures the beauty of her dreams.

It is a thing that brings a man to life. It is one for which many men would die.

A woman's heart is deep, provocative, mesmerizing.

Everything cold and hard about a man, the sculpted stone on the ledge, she contrasts. She *moves*. Her heart is paradoxical to his. Such unspeakable difference, not relative sameness or bland "personhood," becomes too much for him. It *stirs* him to life. In a way he never could be, she is profoundly...beautiful.

And he is entranced. He is inspired to become more of a man. Ready to leap for her furthest dreams as they float by.

She has dropped her teddy, climbed onto the ledge, and revealed herself to him.

And he will ever be in awe.

Can I more aptly describe a woman's beauty and her relationship to a man than this?

FEMININITY: THE EVIDENCE

God is inherently feminine. Now, hold up. Not in the same way he is masculine. As husbands and wives represent

Christ and the church, so God is masculine in relation to his people. He is Father. But women are the image of God, as well.

It is my belief that, although God is masculine in relation to us, the *image* of God is perfectly reflected through the combination of the masculine and feminine images of man and woman. That means who a woman is and what is true about her is just as true about God. It means, just as a man, she reflects him. She reveals him.

So what is it that defines a woman? The feminism of the late 20th and early 21st centuries has had a huge impact on men and women and has redefined our cultural views of them. However, it has possibly had the greatest effect on women. Gender confusion, frustration with men, competing desires for relationships, family, and careers, and a misguided sense of self-actualization have caused mass turmoil in femininity.

In truth, the feminist movement, which sought to re-invent womanhood, started with women. Therefore, the understanding of what it means to be a woman, even by women in this culture, has been greatly damaged.

But God's view is intact. Women are designed with femininity. Who they are matches perfectly with masculinity. It's that simple.

As a society we've lost that.

We think men and women are more or less the same. A few biological differences. A few cultural traditions. And even if the Bible says they're different, it's only in minor ways.

That couldn't be more wrong.

Men and women are intrinsically different. Everything from their biological make-up to the psychology of how they think and the ways they act contrast. They were designed that way.

They have different natures.

We've worked so hard to make women mirror images of men that in the shuffle we've lost who women *were created to be*. Therefore, we've lost the true heart of who women are, as God intends. We've lost the image of God they reflect.

Yet, like so much else, it's simple. They are complex, no doubt, but they are the perfect match to men.

Remember, they were created to help meet. God isn't a sick god who makes people generally the same, but arbitrarily chooses one for one role and dooms the other to a mismatching role.

Focusing on roles misses the point, anyway, because God is about design. Only after it can we understand his plan.

See, design is functional. It makes sense. As a mechanical engineer designs a prototype and tests and fine-tunes it to perform a task, God thoughtfully developed man and woman as two prototypes, perfectly matched for uniquely important tasks. After observing his prototypes and their interweaving abilities with ultimate satisfaction in the lab, God let out a sigh and decided it was very good.

Very good isn't identical creatures with one in charge and the other doing laundry. It isn't spiritual nepotism that rejects qualifications. Very good is two designs for two different purposes, fitting together very well. And, as it was for God, it should be deeply satisfying for each to follow, in a way no other would be.

That is exactly God's plan. For man and woman, it is wondrously pleasing to live out who God made us. It is very good.

THE HEART OF THE MATTER

So what is unique about a woman? Most strikingly, it is her beauty.

A man's strength protects this profound beauty—of intelligence, personality, heart, dreams, and physically splendid form—a beauty of a uniquely feminine and breathtaking kind.

The strength of a man, properly used, encourages it, provides it an environment in which to *thrive*. That is the purpose of godly strength. It's really all about beauty. And in response, her beauty and heart give him life.

She empowers and impassions. Softens and inspires. Nourishes and cares. She moves him and gives life meaning. She is the heart behind the muscle.

The Beauty behind the Beast.

But a woman is much more.

If the world needs warriors to attack and defend, it also needs healers to patch them up. Since men can be mission-focused, they often miss details. However, it is in a woman's nature to notice them. And to care. Women nurture what men often neglect.

Worlds of meaning are wrapped up in this. It's why a woman wants to talk about her day and why she judges her relationship by how close she feels to her man. It's the reason she'd often rather share updates on friends' lives than have theological debates, but would drop either to hug someone who's hurting.

A man is a leader, strategist, and idea-former. She is a lover, nurturer, and heart-giver.

It's no surprise a young woman I know refused to make friends when she learned she'd be moving in six months. There is something deeply sensitive within her. Most guys would make a friend for a day just to have a weightlifting partner.

By nature, a woman is gifted relationally more than a man, with sensitivity to recognize and understand another's pain. And it makes perfect sense. Tenderness and nurture, besides beauty, are the perfect complement to strength and authority.

In this, she's a life-saver who rushes to the rescue. She comes alongside others, and in their pain, she heals. This is perhaps the most remarkable quality of a woman's beauty. Her tender heart gives life.

In our home, my mom was the heart of the family. We beat according to the pulse of her love and kindness. She would pull us close when we fell off our bikes or weren't invited to a friend's birthday party. Her love lifted us.

I still vividly recall my mom putting her hand on my head and praying for my day as I rushed out the door for school each morning. Words cannot express the security I felt in those moments.

A family is nothing without a woman's heart, her intuition and sensitivity. It is breath filling thirsty lungs. In its most enchanting, delicate form, it is love.

A woman's abilities are part of her wondrous design—she is a life-bringer. There is meaning in how my wife decorates each room with care and thought and isn't content until our entire house is a comfortable, cozy home.

She has a gift to uniquely care. To notice. To nurture. To love.

THE PROVERBS 31 COMPLIMENT

Traditional stereotypes have done an injustice to women, but anyone who can't see their intellectual prowess needs to take a brain scan. Or discuss classical composers with my mom. In multiple languages like my wife.

It's no surprise the Proverbs 31 woman does *everything*. She creates with her hands. She buys and prepares food...in the middle of the night. She is productive in real estate. She trades for profit in business. She provides for the poor of the community. She clothes her family. She quilts. She makes clothes to sell. She makes fashion accessories. She watches over the affairs of her household.

Let's consider these more closely. She is an innovator in business—trading, buying, and selling. She is an innovator in fashion—making sashes and clothing for the market. She cares for the needs of her community, mindful of social issues. All this she does while feeding and clothing her family, mostly with what she has made. This is an incredibly intelligent, gifted woman.

Some women see Proverbs 31 as a pressure, an impossible standard to live up to. Really, it's a compliment. God created women with the ability to do all of these. It should be clear women are not inferior to men in any way.

The woman's husband is mentioned in the passage only once. He sits with the elders at the city gate, a man of influence. That isn't to say men should lounge around while their wives do all the work. Rather, this is a picture of a woman who brings great blessing to her family. It is a picture of the power of womanhood.

Her husband sits with the elders because he is leading the community and church, as is his nature. But the message of this passage is the value a godly woman's intelligence and abilities bring to her husband, family, and community.

She is irreplaceable and worthy of great honor. She is "worth far more than rubies" (Prov. 31:10). It is a great loss to minimize her influence in her family, church, and world.

The Hebrew word for "help meet" God uses to describe women is used for one other person in the Bible—the Holy Spirit. And like the Holy Spirit, women are life-savers.

STIRRING WITHIN DEEP WATERS

However, a woman's power is quite different from a man's. It is a power that enchants. One that brings to life. Is it any surprise she shares this distinction with the Holy Spirit?

This is contrary to a man's strength. His is one of brute force, which fits with initiative and authority. Women, on the other hand, have been known to withstand great pain, not on the field of battle, but through the determination and grit of bringing forth a life and holding together a family. A woman's power is less visible than a man's; it is more inward. It comes from her heart.

The obvious example is carrying a child. When my wife delivered our son, Luke, it was the most surreal experience of our lives. I was blown away by how *tough* she was. After nineteen hours of labor (we chose not to use an epidural)—change that—*back* labor, we were the parents of a handsome, active little boy. I felt she needed a week-long cruise after the trauma of it.

When I mentioned this, she abruptly responded, "A month." But instead, two hours after the family trailed off and we finally slipped to bed (at 4:30AM), she was up feeding him. Actually, she stayed awake the whole night. She slept three hours total the first three nights, too anxious to take her eyes off our baby.

I slept like a rock. Every time I awoke for a feeding, it felt like my brain had been morphed into a dishrag, squeezed out, dried in a twisted clump, and asked to do quadratic math.

I couldn't even remember why I existed. I'm pretty sure some of those feedings I didn't wake up at all. Yes, there is something remarkably strong about a woman, and what drives her hints at what is central to who she is.

These deep things of a woman, at their essence, reveal her nature. I suppose the waters of a woman's heart are deeper and more compelling than a man's. For to drink of them brings life.

During family prayer times at our house, my mom would often become quiet for a moment and pick up her Bible. Flipping through the pages, she'd settled on one. We always knew a sensitive word from God's heart would follow. We'd relish it.

This was the source of beauty and love that nourished us as a family. It was stirring within her deep waters.

Similarly, on vacations in northern Michigan, Mom occasionally ventured off for prayer walks into the woods to listen to God's heart. Usually, she'd return with a simple vision or prophecy God wanted to speak to one of us. And his love confirmed in it a message we realized we desperately needed to hear.

Being with Mom gave a sense of being drawn in by loving arms that surrounded us. Her embrace was a place of sensitivity, a place of security.

I think of Jesus lamenting, "Oh Jerusalem, Jerusalem...how often I have longed to gather your children together, as a hen gathers her chicks under her wings...." (Matt. 23:37).

There is something special about the heart of a woman. She is the image of God. She reveals him. As a hen gathers her chicks under her wings.

With Mom, we were comforted, nurtured, cared for. Dad made us feel tough. Mom made us feel safe.

This nature is something a man can never be. His deep waters are different. In hers are reflected the deep heart of God. A man may be tender with his strength, but he will never be this compelling, this emotively powerful.

Her power comes from her deep, compassionate heart.

That is a "help-meet." It is crucial. It is an awesome force in the family. Like the Holy Spirit, it is a life-bringer. It transforms from the inside out. In the face of the world's coldest realities, it *feels*. It beckons, comforts, and in that most important place, it saves. That is a woman.

Who could want to be more?

In the next chapter, we will take a deeper look at what is written on the feminine heart and how it is reflected in God's Word. God's message is quite different from what the world has told her. It may surprise you, but it will certainly unveil the compelling worth it is to be a godly woman.

For her heart is indeed worth far more than rubies.

Overwhelming enough to mesmerize the world, but selfless enough to offer itself to a little child. A woman's heart is wondrously feminine. It is the deepest and most profound waters I know.

Chapter Five
THE THREAD

My wife can charm anything. I think it's a superhuman power, actually. Wonder Woman had bracelets and a lasso. My wife has a sweet, disarming, infinitely less tacky, Crocodile Dundee-like power over animals. She pads up to cats and dogs, any animal, domestic or wild, and puts them in a trance.

At a local mini-golf course, she edged her hand into a parrot's cage and it purred as she rubbed its head.

I bumbled over and it snapped at me. I almost lost fingers while she had it eating out of the palm of her hand. There's something to this. She says it's a skill she thinks everyone should learn. Maybe she's right. But tenderness emanates from her that I can't imitate.

I see this connection in her and my mom. My brother Doy, a former Marine, loves to lie on the couch and have Mom run her fingers through his hair. I don't think he would feel the same way about Dad.

Whether mother or daughter, single or wife, there is a thread that runs through all women. It is beautiful and sensitive. It is resilient. It can be stretched, but not broken. It is tough. Yet, its purpose is to tie people together.

Don't be fooled. It is not flimsy. Women will go through incredible pain and sacrifice for the ones they love. It's no surprise they were chosen to bear and bond with children. A force of compassion and love was written in their DNA. It is powerful and irreplaceable. In addition to childbirth, observe the way they serve their families daily.

And the thread is not to be underestimated. Threaten a mother's children and face her wrath. The strand is strong.

But its defining characteristic is its fascinatingly beautiful, exquisite fiber. And it, in turn, beautifies.

That's something I know. I see enough that I am amazed by a woman more than I understand her. In many ways, she is beyond me.

But I know she is crucial. The world cannot live without her and neither can I.

A woman can charm a wild animal with her tenderness. She can quiet a man as she runs her fingers through his hair. She holds that power in the palm of her hand. She holds it in her heart.

THE DISTORTED IMAGE

But there is a woman who will destroy men with this power. There is another who doesn't believe in it at all.

Proverbs 7 tells of the seductive woman who uses her charm indiscriminately:

> With persuasive words she led him astray; she seduced him with her smooth talk. All at once he followed her like an ox going to the slaughter, like a deer stepping into a noose till an arrow pierces his liver, like a bird darting into a snare, little knowing it will cost him his life. (21-23)

The power of the adulterous woman's beauty is real. If used sexually for anyone other than her husband, it is deathly seductive. So many women use this power to manipulate, seduce, or even boost their own self-esteem. They flip their design from a "help meet" to a "help kill." Women who flaunt sexiness fall into this trap. God wants them to reserve the awesomeness of its fulfillment for his timing *with their hus-*

bands. Otherwise, it is disastrous for men, but also for them, making murky what God intends to be deep, pure waters.

The opposite is just as dangerous. My heart goes out to the hurting woman who doesn't believe she is beautiful. She can't see her sexiness. A girl within cries, believing she is unnoticed by the world. My wife and I watched a show a few days ago about a woman who wore tacky, dumpy clothing because she didn't believe she was attractive. During a make-over, she laughed, giggled, and cried at the beauty a bit of attention revealed in her. By the end, she was a confident, new woman. Like Cinderella.

Every woman goes through phases. Feelings rise and fall with outfits, pregnancies, and schedules of the month. But beauty never changes. It is something God has crafted into femininity. It's part of the thread; every woman is inherently beautiful. And if a woman has a little confidence it seeps through her *pores*. She just has to see herself that way. She may not feel it when she's wearing rags and mopping the kitchen. But every woman is a Cinderella. *Even when she's not wearing the slipper.* It's true. And the more she believes it, the more the fairy tale shines through her.

THE QUIET, GENTLE SPIRIT

At times, the fairy tale meets real life. The beauty and enchantment of femininity transform a group of individuals into a family. A house into a home. Its well of love nourishes the nations or a child who needs a pack lunch and a kiss on the cheek. But being a "help meet" isn't only a source of life; it's a functional role of support, as well. Deeply woven into it is help for another's lead—that of her husband.

My mom understood this as my brothers and I grew up. She made it a personal goal to honor my father's leadership in the family.

At times, as any couple, they disagreed. One particular disagreement was over how to discipline the kids. But she was careful not to question his leadership in front of us. They talked in private. She knew fighting with him would undermine his authority in our family, and, perhaps more importantly, our perception of our dad. I've always respected how she followed Dad's lead and unconditionally supported it.

A couple years ago, she told us how easy it would've been to be the "good guy" by sharing his faults behind his back or explaining why she didn't agree with decisions he'd made. It would've been easy to connect.

But it also would've alienated us from Dad. It most likely would've created insecurities in us because of the divided front between our parents, as well. And while being quietly manipulative, it would have robbed us of the picture of a godly woman respecting and submitting to her husband that we saw in Mom.

I do remember seeing their interactions, though. I saw how she honored him. I saw how he loved her. And I felt very secure as a child.

I am extremely grateful to my mom for this picture, as well as for the way she nurtured our family. I have a much clearer understanding of the heart of femininity because of her. I've read the verses, but I've also seen them applied in everyday life. I saw in her a quality I learned was precious in God's sight and crucial to a woman. I saw her peace submitting to proper leadership.

This isn't something God requests. It is intrinsic to godly femininity.

As a man is designed to lead, a woman is designed to follow.

And she is at peace with it.

This striking quality of a godly woman is referred to in 1 Peter 3: 3-6. The context is Paul speaking to women about submitting to their husbands. He writes:

> Your beauty should not come from outward adornment, such as elaborate hairstyles and the wearing of gold jewelry or fine clothes. Rather, it should be that of your inner self, the unfading beauty of a gentle and quiet spirit, which is of great worth in God's sight. For this is the way the holy women of the past who put their hope in God used to adorn themselves. They submitted themselves to their own husbands, like Sarah, who obeyed Abraham and called him her lord. You are her daughters if you do what is right and do not give way to fear. (1 Peter 3:3-6)

The quality so many miss is the gentle, quiet spirit. It is a definitive quality of a woman of God. It doesn't mean a quiet woman. She isn't huddled in a corner without a personality. It is a woman who is at peace with following her husband. She trusts him. It shows she has peace in her soul with God. She has determined in her heart God will protect her. The matter is settled. She trusts God.

The shocking part is this passage is instructing women who don't even have believing husbands to trust and submit. That is the strength of true femininity. In the face of any outcome, when life is out of her hands, a woman of God has a "quiet spirit" before her husband and before God. She does not "give way to fear."

The opposite of this is controlling and manipulating. This is perhaps women's greatest temptation. Since God put authority in the hands of men, women often find themselves trying to control it. The quiet spirit is probably the most important quality for them to disciple in their daughters. It is one of trust, and it totally changes a woman's behavior toward her husband.

Manipulation, taking matters into her own hands, keeping issues from her husband, or trying to control his decision-making are the opposite of this quality. They give way to fear. They are the antitheses to God's design for femininity.

That is why, when I recognized this quiet, gentle spirit in a young woman a few years ago, I knew I'd found an amazing woman. I saw her peace with God and authority. I knew this was of great worth in God's sight. It has become of increasing worth to me in the weeks and months since I've married her.

I delight in Angela. She is an extremely beautiful woman. I love staring into her pretty, green eyes. I am often amazed when I look at her. But there is an unfading beauty in her no hairstyle, jewelry, or clothing can imitate. That is what Paul is getting at. So many women try to achieve beauty through expensive clothes, eye shadow, and "outward adornment"; they are caught up with an imitation that isn't them and can't connect with true beauty.

A woman's spirit, however, is transparent. One can easily read what she expresses about herself and her relationship with God and men. The femininity of the woman of adultery in Proverbs 7 is seductive, as well as her fashionable clothes, jewelry, elaborate hairstyles, and, most notably, the brazen look in her eyes. Admittedly, it's pretty common in our culture. But it is far from femininity as God intended it. It can't touch true beauty.

Don't underestimate the woman of quiet, gentle spirit. She is not dull. She is beautiful. She is seductive *to her husband*. She flashes her own unique personality. She is full of life. She is the talented Proverbs 31 woman. She is so spectacular she is called "the glory of man." And yet she reserves this spectacle for her husband.

Instead, she emanates priceless beauty from a heart that follows her husband's lead and trusts him as she trusts the Lord.

What a picture of beauty. What profound quietness and strength. Deep waters set with a picturesque fountain, flowing to eternal life. This is the peace of a godly woman. And it is my great delight.

A NATURE TO FOLLOW

The thread of a woman's femininity weaves even deeper. Her nature is revealed in an oft-told story.

A woman moved away from town with her two sons. Both sons married and eventually died, and their mother prepared to return home. When the time came to leave, her two daughters-in-law chose to go with her. She was shocked they would willingly leave everything they knew, their families and culture, to be with her. The mother-in-law urged them to stay with their homes and families. Finally, one turned back. The other spoke these remarkable, famous words:

> Where you go I will go, and where you stay I will stay. Your people will be my people and your God my God. Where you die I will die, and there I will be buried. May the LORD deal with me, be it ever so severely, if anything but death separates you and me.
> (Ruth 1:16b,17)

Her name was Ruth.

The example she gives is an exquisite picture of femininity. She goes where the lead goes. She stays, gladly, where it stays. Nothing will keep her from following. She would die before rejecting the opportunity to do so. What beauty, so wholeheartedly accepting a lead.

And this nature fits magnificently with what we've seen. Man was created with authority, strength, and decisive logic and is designed to lead. Woman was created with a deep heart, beauty, and nurturing sensitivity and is designed to help the lead. To give it life.

Both require intelligence and character to fulfill their designs. Both are essential; together they form the perfect partnership.

As with Ruth, matching the lead means being willing to adapt. *Your people will be my people.* She's willing to follow with everything she has, even her heart and allegiance. *Your God, my God.* Her life's purpose is receptive and comes alongside another's.

Those who argue Ruth was following her mother-in-law, not a man, miss the point. This isn't a lesson about how daughters should follow mothers-in-law. It isn't a lesson about how non-Christians should follow Christians, either. At its simplest, this is an example of a woman who is living out what is truly natural about being a woman. And she is blessed for it. What is definitive is not to whom, but *what* she is doing. She is revealing herself.

She is no push-over. But she instinctively knows she is created to follow. It is natural.

Like breathing in and breathing out.

With this insight, many brides make these words their wedding vows. How precious that is in the sight of God. Look at the thread of femininity throughout Scripture and you'll see how this exemplifies the heart of a godly woman.

Sarah follows Abraham, unquestioningly calling herself his sister because of his fear of jealous locals. She goes so far as obeying him and is praised in the New Testament for it.

Abigail, Nabal's wife, shows the same deference for David. Her quick reactions protect her husband from insulting him, but the Lord causes Nabal to die of a heart attack, anyway. Her wisdom and sharpness attract David to her. Still, when she receives an offer to marry him, her response is, "Here is your maidservant, ready to serve you and wash the feet of my master's servants" (1 Sam. 25:41).

Later in her own story, Ruth makes her intent clear to Boaz by slipping under the corner of his blanket. She communicates her reliance on him. Putting herself at his feet is a sign of adopting his lead.

Even Esther, the hero who saves the nation of Israel in time of crisis, gives herself completely to the king and honors his headship in contrast to the previous queen, winning him over by her breathtaking beauty, but also, unmistakably, her submission.

These are amazing women. They are intelligent, gifted, wise, courageous, sharp, faithful, talented, and beautiful—as honored as any women of God. But when it comes to their relationships with their husbands, each chooses to go where he goes and stay where he stays. This is a mark of true femininity.

With a quiet, gentle spirit, each delights in the husband God has given to provide her security, and in that place, under the corner of his blanket, she finds freedom.

RECLAIMING DESIGN

This isn't the model relationship of the modern-day church, however. Our pattern is more...vague. Usually, two partners co-exist in a blend of relationship dynamics, with extreme final decisions made by the husband. Godly masculinity and femininity are mostly misunderstood, so the picture of our relationships remains incomplete.

Yet, since they are crucial to a healthy marriage, is it any wonder so many Christian marriages are falling apart?

God's design is clear and practical.

Men and women have different natures. They are evident around us, from the imaginations of little boys to the dreams of little girls. From men who stand up to fight to women who rush in to nurture them. It is the way of God's world. And it is written in God's Word.

One leads. The other follows. One marks the way. The other gives it meaning. They were designed that way.

The leader does not lord it over the beloved. He empowers his wife's dreams. He listens to her, knowing she has crucial insights and intuition. He analyzes, thinks, and plans the best for the family. As a wise leader, he honors his wife's invaluable abilities and puts her first, but he is never passive. The responsibility to lead the whole family is his. He has been created for this purpose.

The follower does not manipulate or control. She trusts her husband's leadership and wisdom. She nurtures and cares beside him. She uplifts and restores. As a wise follower, she respects her husband's direction, but she is never invalidated. She plays a crucial, life-saving role of nourishment, support, insight, and love to her family. This responsibility is hers. She has been created for this purpose.

And they fit marvelously together. Leader and follower. Strength and beauty. Authority and nurturer. Decision-maker and life-saver.

Man and woman.

Knowing God's design allows us to live out our natures in a God-pleasing way. Only then can we embrace our places in the family and church and understand God's Word on the subject.

The world says men are uncontrollable, and women are worth little until they become like men.

It is wrong. Men *must* be men, the godly ones sacrificing everything for their wives as Christ did. And women *must* be women. Who they are brings infinite glory to God. In view of their profound beauty and life-giving nature, who would not want to be a woman?

Awesome and beautiful, an image reflecting the sensitive, deep heart of God, woman is glorious in a way man never could be.

And she is irreplaceable. The perfect complement to the fierceness of man is her captivating heart.

"The purposes of a man's heart are deep waters, but a man of understanding draws them out" (Prov. 20:5).

This is true of woman. So much in these deep places tells of a uniquely intimate, yet masterfully complex Beauty. The secret of her mystique is femininity. It balances creation. Breathtaking, alluring, tender, inspiring, life-saving, and awesome.

Together man and woman were charged to rule over the earth and subdue it. The man to lead and she to bring to life at his side. Together these two natures cannot be paralleled.

The world has not seen anything like them. It holds its breath.

And stands back in wonder.

Chapter Six-
BREATHING IN AND BREATHING OUT

I suck in shallow breaths as I tighten my grip around the stroller handles and force one foot in front of the other. It's been a long time since I worked out, and my body barely remembers.

My heels hit the pavement with impacts just strong enough to settle all my joints into position to being useful again.

And it feels good. Luke quietly takes in the trees and grass and breeze as a curious new observer to this world, while the jogger wheels gently whir along the road.

Who am I kidding? Luke is probably checking out the gutter or rubber on some car's tires, or contemplating the mystery of looking up and seeing blue.

But this is the right place to be in the world.

Mom was worn out from nursing (I call it milking), so the boys decided to get a little exercise.

Fifteen steps is all I need to realize this will take some work. My Schwinn jogger is a top of the line model that looks more like a Formula One racing car than a stroller. It swallows Luke in a cockpit (yes, cockpit) with long straps, inches above wide rubber tires that beg for speed.

I give it all I have.

As we race (crawl) along, I think back on the whirlwind Angela and I passed through the last year. Married with fanfare that spilled out of a jubilant reception hall, a surprise destination honeymoon in cliff-side huts overlooking the ocean, cave-diving, perfect white sand beaches, horseback riding along the shore, a sneak preview of a surprise guest, and now, ten months later, the most adorable one month old stock stroller driver and a Schwinn with high performance wheels and adjustable road settings.

And it feels right.

It's been wild, unpredictable, excruciating at times, and most of all, incomparably romantic. I wouldn't have it any other way.

Though my life has changed dramatically in the last year, from single to married to parenthood, the balance of where I now find myself…fits.

On numerous occasions, Angela and I have been called a great team. It started when we led a young adult's group—she the girls and I the guys—before we dated. It carried on as we worked through the labor pains of our son.

If true, the reason we're a great team is because, like any other, we know our positions. We embrace them. One reason I considered dating Angela early on was I saw how easily she fit as a godly woman to a man of God. We worked and communicated together, but she naturally fell in step behind my lead. That's somewhat of a rare thing today.

It's what God intends.

Together man and woman can be a great team, a winning combination. But they have to know and embrace their places on it. They have to understand and accept *who they are*.

The balance comes in how well they fit their opposing natures together. It isn't too different from inhaling and exhaling to draw long, full, deep breaths.

Like me, here, huffing as I try to keep up with Luke and his Dukes of Hazard muscle stroller.

You see, God's remarkable balance—his romantic, whirlwind love story for mankind—isn't simply intended for fun, actualization, or entitlement. No, it produces something much more satisfying—*life*.

Something I appreciate as I take another turn down the street with my newborn son.

THE RIGHT MAP

Often, the church doesn't understand how this balance works. So, little by little, we allow the culture to influence us. The result depolarizes our natures and leaves men and women in a dreary, uninspiring state of sameness. It robs what God made sweepingly romantic about our relationship.

One example of this comes from Ephesians.

Ephesians 5:21 says, "Submit to one another out of reverence for Christ." The passage then outlines relationships that submit.

First, wives to husbands. "Wives submit to your husbands as to the Lord" (v.22). Paul elaborates on this.

Next come children and parents. "Children obey your parents in the Lord, for this is right" (6:1).

He isn't finished. "Slaves obey your earthly masters...just as you would obey Christ" (6:5).

The mistake many Christians make is to interpret the first line of "[submitting] to one another" as mutual, as though everyone submits to everyone else, wives to husbands—and husbands to wives—in different circumstances. But why then would Paul specifically tell wives to submit?

Still, some teach that women primarily submit, but the *way* men lead is by submitting. This just confuses everything.

Think through that circular reasoning for a moment. Could you imagine telling a general, "You are to lead your troops and they are to submit to you. However, the way you lead is by submitting to them..."? I can see the glassy-eyed stares now. No wonder men and women are so disoriented.

What they are confusing is submission and sacrifice. Submission is a position of being under another in authority. Sacrifice is using authority to love.

Christ sacrificed on the cross. He didn't submit to the church, but to the Father above him. He led it. Neither does a husband submit to his wife when he lays his life down. He submits to the Father, but he always has ultimate responsibility to lead her. And with it he loves.

The simple meaning of the passage is people submit to each other. But not *every* person to *every* other. The first line is the theme. The next are the explanations.

If we understand the meaning of the word "submit"—to put oneself under authority—and the analogy of a husband to his wife as Christ is to the church, can there really be any other interpretation?

Yet, in the confusion, men are left wandering without a map to point the way written on their hearts—how to be leaders, how to be men.

If we don't have the right directions, we are in serious trouble.

THE HOUSEHOLD OF GOD

Many of us understand a few directions from God. Yet, the path is hard to make out. For example, most Christian men know:

1. The man is the head of the house
2. He should be a servant leader
3. He makes final decisions in the family

Somehow, that isn't enough to explain his nature. Nor does it teach him *how* to be an effective man of God. Something has to dip into his deep waters. What's in a man's heart to teach him of his place in his home, church, and greater purpose? What connects with his desires? There has to be more.

And there is.

If someone were to break down the game of football to you in a few steps, you could get the gist of how to play. You might hear a talk or two, regurgitating ideas with a clever story to carry the application across. It would be enough to yell at the TV.

How to be a successful football player

1. Throw the ball—pull your arm back, snap it forward, release
2. Catch the ball—extend your arms and grab it
3. Tackle—wrap your arms around the ball carrier and drag him to the ground

Based on such a training model, how successful would a football team be? Not very. Certainly not ready to win a national championship or Super Bowl. But take a look at how we often prepare men in church:

1. Listen to an overview in a sermon
2. Hear a couple stories
3. Now go do it

But there's a lot more.

Like in football, we can be trained to become a national championship team. So well-trained we *are destined to win.*

The church usually does things differently, though. We lift free weights on Sunday and go for a jog on Wednesday. The more serious work out by themselves every day.

Yet still we expect to win the championship?

In 2007, Alabama football coach Nick Saban took over for the previous head coach, who finished 6-7 and was fired. The first year, he led his team to a 7-6 season with a 4-4 conference record.

Two years later they won the national championship.

The truth is Saban knew how to train a championship team. The team's success didn't happen by accident. There was never any doubt they would reach it. And Saban has proved it with multiple championships.

That's as true spiritually as in any other area.

Haphazard training in an inefficient system doesn't win championships. Businesses, sports, and organizations give us clues. It's the wisdom built into the foundation of the world.

I sometimes wonder whether the church thinks spiritual growth happens by osmosis. Throw out some seed on a Sunday morning and the Holy Spirit does all the work. Yet few Christians reach maturity by their senior year and the church isn't winning any championships.

But it should be.

The reality is life in Christ isn't a mystical sphere that transforms without the training. It's incredibly practical. That's why Paul says, "We proclaim him, admonishing and teaching everyone *with all wisdom*, so that we may present everyone perfect in Christ" (Col. 1:28, emphasis mine).

We use all wisdom to mature everyone to perfection in Christ. Strong at our positions. Like the dominant linebacker. The freakish offensive lineman. The championship within reach.

That's the purpose of the church.

Like a national championship team, the church must be honed as an efficient training system with "players" who are taught their positions. Trust me; I'm not removing the spiritual aspect. The Holy Spirit ignites and causes the growth. But he uses real people and real wisdom to do it. We don't need to be practically undisciplined to allow room for the Holy Spirit. Instead, the opposite is true. Paul uses "all wisdom" as he fully trusts God. He "beats his body...to obtain the prize" (1 Cor. 9:7). We must be well trained and the church must be *efficient* to point the whole team to success. Then we can be bred for the championships.

But first we need a new paradigm.

MAN'S PLACE

To start, we must know our positions. Most men know they have one in the family. Whatever it means, they are the heads of their homes. But largely, they also know they have no place in church.

Some proactive men pass the offering plate or direct cars in the parking lot. Others become prayer partners or lead worship. But most don't see themselves *responsible* for the church. Elders are often the exception. Still, it should be remarkable most men don't feel personally responsible for the health of the family of God. This is the result of a church structure that leaves pastors bearing the weight of the church alone.

Let that sink in.

God designed half of creation—every man—with a specific skill set for authority, yet hardly any of them see themselves responsible for the church.

And it's our fault.

For many reasons, they've been left out. They have no purpose there. If they volunteer, they can serve as chair stackers or door greeters. In business one would say, "There's nowhere to go but up from there," with a wink and a smile. We know Jesus came "not to be served, but to serve" and we should do the same. However, we are in serious trouble if the church isn't designed for men to do much more. Though its needs are huge, there are noticeably few opportunities for true authority in the church for those who *have been made for it.*

And that is a serious problem.

Our cultural view of good men is Little League fathers but armchair church members. The domain of a man of God ends at the doors of the church. His calling isn't found there. Really, the word calling doesn't fit; that's for a man like the pastor. It's where we are now. Men are husbands and have families and that's enough.

But that isn't the way God intended it to be.

There is a calling on every man.

THE CALLING

Every one has a *mission*.

Man's role in church isn't as trivial as he has been led to believe. His "entry level position" is more important than is commonly taught. This lack of teaching is precisely the reason men have walked away from the church in droves. They didn't know what great things they were made for. They were given no vision.

They were never told they could be CEOs, though it was written on their hearts. And no, they could not be team captains or generals, but there wasn't any other place they fit. The common man doesn't feel right merely taking part, listening, and following along. And he shouldn't.

There's a reason he relishes his armchair on Sunday. During the afternoon game, he can analyze, strategize, cast vision, and coach. An exciting venue beckons him to try his talents. The ones he was born for. Sure, it isn't real. But it's an outlet for his design.

And it's the reason he isn't living it in church.

He doesn't see how his nature fits there.

Have you ever thought about what the word husband means? It comes from the Old English, husbonda, which means master of a house. Its meaning today, besides "male partner in a marriage" is a manager, a steward.

As husbands, men are more than male partners in a marriage. They are head managers, masters of God's house. Even single men have the nature of masculinity. They were designed with authority.

For this reason, Paul says the husband is the "head of the wife as Christ also is the head of the church" (Eph. 5:24). Then, he instructs husbands to:

> Love your wives, just as Christ also loved the church and gave himself up for her, to make her holy, cleansing her by the washing with water through the word, that he might present to himself the church in all her glory, having no spot or wrinkle or any such thing; but that she would be holy and blameless. (Eph. 5:25-27)

Pastors often teach the first verses. "Husbands, love your wives." Love them sacrificially, "as Christ also loved the church and gave Himself up for her." The importance of these verses cannot be overstated. However, in thirty years of regular church attendance, I haven't heard a teaching that goes on.

You see, the husband has a clear purpose with his love. It is to cleanse his wife. He is to wash her with water through the Word. Let that sink in. The water of the Word. Whose job does that sound like?

That's right. That's the pastor's job.

In millions of churches around the world, a man will stand up and deliver what many consider the primary ministry of church. He will teach the ministry of the Word. He will cleanse his congregation.

This is not an accidental illustration in Ephesians. It is an allusion.

Its origin is in the final prayer and instruction of the Man to whom this whole passage is relating husbands—Jesus.

After the Last Supper, before Jesus was betrayed, he looked around the table and said:

> I am the true vine and my Father is the vinedresser. Every branch in me that does not bear fruit he takes away;

and every branch that bears fruit he prunes, that it may bear more fruit. *You are already clean because of the word which I have spoken to you.* (John 15:1-3, emphasis mine)

"Cleansing her by the washing with water through the word."

"Clean because of the word which I have spoken to you."

The similarities should jump out at you. The husband is to do for his wife exactly what Jesus did for his disciples.

The ministry of the Word in a church is more than teaching. It's discipleship. It presents the church to himself in all her glory. It takes the body, no matter how small or big, and cleanses it 'til she has no spot or wrinkle. Until she is holy and blameless.

We use words like sanctification. Jesus said clean them with the Word until they're blameless. He did it for his disciples. He passed that ministry on to them and told them to do likewise.

And men, he gave that same ministry to you for your wives.

God made each man a pastor.

That's right, as much as any pastor in any church. A pastor. With a pastor's responsibilities, even a pastor's job title—husbonda—master of a house. Husband. Designed for leadership, bred for authority.

The perfect prototype for a mission. From the creation of the world, he was destined to be a unique hero with a hero's calling.

We idolize film heroes because they are ordinary men who realize extraordinary destinies. They speak to our hearts. But they are merely shadows that hint to what is inside us.

We are the ones with true heroism in our DNA, with a masculine code that runs as deep as the heart of man itself. We were made for a purpose. It is reflected in our hearts and dreams and heroes. It calls to us. And this is one call it's time to answer.

Like it or leave it, the moment a man promised to cherish a woman "'til death do you part," he was also *called*. As much as any pastor, he was called. And he has a congregation that needs him. Authority. Not an ego boost or a shot in the arm. But real authority.

Like Jonah or the pastor of a church, a man cannot rescind this call. His wife and his children's lives are in his hands to shepherd, to lead, and to disciple. She is not the pastor's congregation. She is his.

PASTORS AND CHURCH AUTHORITY

Whoa, whoa, whoa. Hold on. The pastor is the head of the church. He is the real authority over men and women, right?

Well, he has authority. God is a God of order, not chaos, and his church must be ordered. In regard to church leadership, Hebrews 13:7 says, "Remember those who led you, who spoke the word of God to you; and considering the result of their conduct, imitate their faith." Our leaders are examples to us. We learn from them.

And later, in verse 17, "Obey your leaders and submit to them, for they keep watch over your souls as those who will give an account. Let them do this with joy and not with grief, for that would be unprofitable for you" (NASB).

We are to follow honorable men who lead the church. They are held accountable for teaching and discipling. Everyone, including men, is instructed to submit to their leaders in church. Paul also implies we should only follow leaders whose conduct is exemplary, like Jesus's. *Considering the result of their conduct.*

An organization whose leaders are ignored is ineffective. Imagine a business with renegade employees who break office policies and undermine the work environment. It will not last long.

The same is true of church. Pastors run the church and empower mature Christians. We listen to them to grow in maturity, as long as we discern their teaching lines up with the Word of God. They have a vital role in encouraging faith. But their final authority doesn't extend beyond the church organization. They don't dictate to anyone, just as the president of a company doesn't tell an employee how to run his personal life.

Years ago, my dad was approached by a church leader. He apologized for any bad advice he may have given over the years. It was a blanket apology with no real basis. The church was going through some upheaval and he hoped to cover any mistakes in his counsel. To his amazement, my dad refused. He said, "No, I will not accept your apology, because I am a man of God. Any choice I made was my own and I made it as a man. You gave advice and it was my decision whether or not to follow it." The man was blown away. He laughed and relented.

Those words were directly on point.

A pastor of a church does not have authority over his congregants' lives. His advice is helpful and formative. He has authority in the church setting. They are to be respectful, grow from his instruction, and follow humbly to promote church order and make his ministry a joy. But the responsibility to direct their lives is entirely their own. They should not accept or submit to his teaching automatically. On a personal level, they must analyze, think, pray, and discern for themselves what God is saying to them. The final authority is theirs.

WHEN TWO BECOME ONE

In a marriage, however, God gives the husband the authority. Husbands and wives communicate and make many decisions together, but the husband is ultimately responsible for their relationship.

Their differences combine in a beautiful, God-ordained fit. Each provides a distinct, crucial role.

When the two play their parts, this stage comes alive with a pageantry too remarkable to call anything but spiritual. It is deeply rooted in the heart of God.

On this stage, only a man can lead. Not the pastor, not the church.

This is the beauty hidden in two becoming one flesh. Do you see Christ and the church in it?

God has offered them this intimacy—to the woman, her husband's love and security, and to the man, his wife's heart and discipleship.

Yet, we devalue the position of this "pastor."

We ignore or manipulate his lead and her love until they look genderless and safe. We neutralize the beauty until nothing is left of God's nature.

My dad used to gaze into my mom's eyes and lavish her with compliments in front of the boys at special dinners. I will never forget how her eyes would light up.

That is how a man leads his wife. With love. With tenderness. With the acknowledgment he couldn't come close to making it without her.

Sarah "obeyed Abraham and called him her lord" (1 Pet. 3:6). Lord to her meant what it sounds like; she followed him and placed her life in his hands.

That is how a woman trusts her husband. Peter says, "You are her daughters if you do what is right and do not give way to fear" (v.6). This fear is of trusting his lead with complete faith as Sarah did.

This beautiful partnership, this love relationship representing God and his Bride, is why a wife trusts her husband's wisdom and leadership even above the pastor of their church. It's God's order.

A pastor once confronted the wife of a friend of mine after a service. He criticized her pointedly, and she was crushed. When her husband found out, he was understandably upset. He disagreed with the advice and how their pastor approached his wife. But most of all, he knew it was out of order. He respectfully told the pastor if something needed to be addressed with his wife to tell him instead. He would decide whether it was appropriate and should be passed along.

The husband was right. This isn't a slam on the pastor, but a deeper look into authority. We need to understand the nature of these relationships.

God has chosen the husband to judge in his family's lives and gently and lovingly lead them in the direction he believes God is leading. This awesome responsibility is his alone. So, actually, a man's authority as pastor of his home is an even stronger relationship than a pastor's over his congregation.

It is God's design. Christ is the head of man. Man, the head of woman.

God created this breathtaking balance. He hid it thoughtfully in the hearts of man and woman. And only a church willing to draw out deep waters will find it.

-Chapter Seven-

IDENTITY CRISIS IN CHURCH

The other day, an epiphany occurred to my mom. We were discussing the difference between the world and the church. She remarked, "You know, we often talk about our witness and how different we are supposed to look from the culture. I think possibly the greatest witness is when strong men in the church can co-exist and not be threatened by each other's strength."

What a church that would be.

Imagine the frightening power of a vast army of fully empowered men living out their nature for the mission of the gospel. Each taking his place.

My brother, Richard, adds that men were not created to be sheep, but formed in the likeness of a lion. That lion is none other than the famous Lion of Judah. Although we are sheep in analogy to our Shepherd, we've also been created with the nature of a lion, like Christ. We are following a lion.

We would have a much different church if we adopted this view.

Men are not meant to simply be followers, to slip into the back and find a place in the masses. We know that; it doesn't add up to what's inside us. We are lions. We've been endowed with the strength of the Lion of Judah. We are leaders, and in our families, we are pastors.

This changes everything.

Now, a man doesn't merely learn from his pastor; he watches how he pastors, and if exemplary, he pastors his home likewise. Now, a church service transforms from a gathering of congregants into a pastors' conference, training to "go and do likewise." When a man hears a sermon, he doesn't simply learn and accept. He analyzes, studies, evaluates, and shapes what he will teach his congregation at home.

He is a leader.

And seeing lower level employees as future presidents is the first way to make business explode. Truly, God designed presidency in them. In the church, God designed authority in the heart of man.

It is the nature of things. It is not the enemy. It will not implode the church. It will not steal pastors' authority. It will support and release it. And if harnessed, it will set the world on fire.

THE BEAUTY OF THE BALANCE

However, when we confuse our natures—when we jumble up our positions—we weaken the church. We ignore what is true about our hearts.

When men withdraw from leadership in church, women feel their absence. They lose the strength of heroic men surrounding and protecting them. They learn men will not come through, will not rescue them; there are no pillars to lean on.

Women were designed to nurture, but not to lead while giving that support. They need men to take their role. And men aren't properly fit for the reverse. They're not nearly the champion lovers and nurturers women are, so when men don't lead they become casualties and their place, a loss.

Similarly, when women take leadership roles meant for men, men become complacent and withdrawn. They pull back, with no place for their leadership gifts and nature to thrive. A twinge in their guts tells them it's not the natural order. They sit in quiet frustration, never living out who God *made* them to be.

Men were designed to lead, but not to deeply, sensitively nurture while doing so. They depend on women for that role. And women aren't properly fit for the reverse. They aren't the broad-scope leaders and strategists men are, and when they abandon uplifting and supporting, everyone feels the loss.

Do you see how the two rely on each other?

The same pattern in the family exists in the church. Men and women fit the same roles in the church as they do in the family because they are the same men and women in each. They have the same *design*. Naturally, they function the same way.

That's why God calls men to teach and pastor in church. Remember, a man is the pastor of his family. So God calls men to pastor the church. In the church, like in the family, discipling and leading are the pastoral roles.

God wants women powerfully active—living out their natures with passion, fulfilling their dreams and purposes in church. He delights in their talents. They are essential. Nothing excites their Father more than seeing their eyes light up as they carry out the desires of their hearts.

In addition, women are essential in leading other women, as well as leading children. That's why, after explaining the qualifications of male leaders over the church in 1 Timothy, Paul instructs the older women to teach the younger women.

And Scripture perfectly supports this balance. The passages about women remaining silent simply point to men leading the church. Head pieces as signs of men's authority while women pray or prophesy are an early church way of displaying it. Not teaching or exercising authority over men is the specific instruction. Classifying overseers and deacons (pastors and elders) as men makes the point clear.

When one sees the directions in church line up perfectly with men and women in the family, it becomes obvious they are the simple products of masculinity and femininity.

GOD'S DESIGN FROM THE BEGINNING

Although it may feel inclusive to have women be pastors and elders or give sermons, women have a unique, godly role that supports the church, makes it *shine*, ministers to it in a way distinctly nurturing and feminine, yet that doesn't undermine men's design as pastors who have the responsibility to disciple the church as they do their families.

Paul touches on this when he says women shouldn't perform these roles—"teach or exercise authority over a man" (1 Tim. 2:12). And it fits the vision of our natures perfectly.

Paul's reason is how God created us, not a sin-filled world that won't accept women, not a cultural bias or stigma in the church, but our *design*.

"For it was Adam who was first created, then Eve" (v.13).

Paul refers to creation to point out our natures, how God designed us to function from the beginning.

The other reason is the fall. "And it was not Adam who was deceived, but the woman being deceived, fell into transgression" (v.14).

Paul doesn't blame Eve for sin. In Romans 5, he blames original sin on Adam. He's explaining women weren't meant to lead men, as Eve did during the fall. Instead, men should lead. That's their nature. And really the reversal was Adam's fault. He was the one who didn't step up and lead her.

DISCERNING TRUTH

Still, some dispute applying masculinity and femininity—our natures—to the church.

They point to references like Priscilla and Aquila or Deborah, a judge, as proof women may pastor.

What they miss is God's use of Deborah supports men's

call to lead. In the story the Bible records of her, she receives a word from God for the king to go into battle. He is afraid to fight without her, so he receives a curse that *the glory would go to a woman.* That's the point. Israel, in its rebellion, has strayed from God's plan. And when no man will step up, listen to God, and lead, a woman should. Deborah, a woman of great courage and sensitivity to God, does and God blesses it richly. Yet these verses clearly support God's desire for men to stand up and lead his people.

In case you doubt this, Isaiah laments later how the nation has drifted, "Youths oppress my people, *women rule over them.* O my people, your guides lead you astray; they turn you from the path" (Is. 3:12, emphasis mine). Isaiah wouldn't lament women leading if God endorses it as a standard practice for the people of God.

Likewise, some claim Priscilla in the New Testament was a pastor because her name is mentioned in order before her husband's, Aquila, in a few of the references to them. "Greet Priscilla and Aquila" (Rom. 16:3). That's it. I didn't realize what an implication I was making every time I've said, "Mom and Dad."

The problem with forming truth from indirect references (interpretations) is if one must ignore direct references—commands—to do so. The reverse is how to interpret Scripture. Always accept direct statements first. Then interpret indirect references within that context. There's no point fighting over whether Deborah shows women may lead when men won't step up or that women may lead men all the time when God's Word later says women shouldn't lead them.

It becomes clear when we start with the right context. In this case, the context is the breathtaking design of masculinity and femininity, the beautiful exchange we've seen from the beginning, and God's specific commands concerning the matter.

GENDER-NEUTRALIZING RAY GUNS

Yet, some scriptures seem unclear to many Christians. Looking deeper, however, illuminates them. One that is often used to gender-zap us with the spiritual ray gun of the new covenant is Galations 3:28. It says, "There is neither Jew nor Greek, slave nor free, male nor female, for you are all one in Christ Jesus." Its meaning becomes clear in light of the verses before and after it:

> Before the coming of this faith, we were held in custody under the law, locked up until the faith that was to come would be revealed....Now that this faith has come, we are no longer under a guardian.
>
> So in Christ Jesus *you are all children of God* through faith, for *all of you* who were baptized into Christ have clothed yourselves with Christ. There is neither Jew nor Gentile, neither slave nor free, nor is there male and female, for you are all one in Christ Jesus. If you belong to Christ, then you are Abraham's seed, and heirs according to the promise. (vv.23-29, emphasis mine)

Some read, "Nor is there male and female," and say, "See, women can do whatever men do in church." But this isn't about our natures, either in the family or the church. The passage makes the meaning clear. It's about how we're all God's kids.

Try applying their interpretation to the other topics in the verse. Paul doesn't mean Jews are no longer Jews. He definitely isn't saying slaves stop being slaves; in Ephesians he tells them to obey their masters as they would the Lord. And this verse doesn't even mention the church, so if one neutralizes men and women in church, one has to do it in the family, too. That means men aren't the heads of their wives as Christ is to the church. It means men and women have no distinctions in marriage. But wisdom (and careful reading) teaches us differently.

Quite simply, this passage isn't about God's order or our natures, at all. It's about the equal promise we all receive in Christ. It's about our inheritance in him.

There isn't a single verse in the Bible that eliminates our natures and positions on his "team." Put down the ray guns. It would never happen. Life in Christ doesn't turn us into spooky, generic, dull spiritual beings.

Not when God created us wonderfully unique. No, the new covenant in Christ restores us to walking with God as we truly are, as men and women, not losing a single, glorious distinction.

Paul is empowering us for this.

REFRIGERATORS, ZEBRAS, AND NATURE

A factory makes products to specification. Machines pump out thousands of exact replicas with surprising accuracy. Imagine the surprise if a refrigerator factory one day produced a jeep.

Or a zebra birthed an antelope.

Refrigerator factories make little plastic applicators that, when pressure is applied, make ice appear. Zebras birth stripes. And the zebras they reproduce don't act like antelopes.

If one wants to carry the analogy further, a line of refrigerators doesn't randomly include parts from a different model. A longer shelf. A slimmer spill tray. A refrigerator would only have different parts if the machine creating them was programmed that way. Otherwise, the foreign parts that slid snugly into place in the original won't match the new model. They'd have to be bent or broken to mash them into a place for which they weren't intended. They wouldn't fit.

Like refrigerators, we shouldn't mash up the pieces to try to fit them into a place for which they weren't intended.

Each part is produced with a purpose.

Shockingly, nature's production is as efficient as the factory. Zebra offspring come out what zebras usually are. A female isn't born with male DNA. With people, too, the parts are pretty much the same. And that's a good thing.

We are wonderfully complex beings. Far more so than refrigerators or zebras. But when we say one can be used in place of the other without the parts or programming, without the design, we're creating an inefficient environment for the products. We're confusing our purposes and will greatly lose productivity.

In the church, we are "God's workmanship," tools for his purpose. "Created in Christ Jesus to do good works, which God prepared in advance for us to do" (Eph. 2:10). His design is the way we best display his glory. We can't afford to lose what God designed about men and women.

Men, those with the nature of authority, must be the authority as pastors and elders in the church, leading courageously as they do in the family. Women, those with the nurturing nature, must uplift, support, and restore there. They must *bring to life*. Only if we live out our true natures can the church be the glorious Beauty God intends her to be.

Do you see how we fit as naturally in the church as we do in the family?

If anyone disagrees, go back to God's theme of humanity starting with creation in Genesis 1, his purposeful instructions to men and women in the family throughout Scripture, his multiple, clear directions about men and women in the church, culminating with his Bride inviting us to come join him in Revelation 22.

Go back to "it was very good."

If we understand who we are, women are honored to be women as God intended, full of glory, wonder, and breathtaking femininity, yet guided by the leadership of the men.

Men are honored to be men as God intended, full of strength, initiative, and fierce masculinity, yet supported by the life-saving power of the women.

In view of this matchless combination, the world is taken aback by the strength of who he is and what he offers. It catches its breath at the beauty of who she is and all she holds. And so does the church.

THE PASTOR
—*Breathing In*—

NAVIGATING THE JOURNEY...

- *Preparing His Heart*
- *Listening and Assessing*
- *Discipling*
- *Relationships with God*
- *Family Relationships*

-Chapter Eight-
STIRRING THE BEAUTY

Preparing His Heart…

This is the point at which we have found ourselves. The church is waiting, like the dunes of northern Michigan along the great lake, where legend tells of a bear who fell asleep beside the waters and was covered with sand that blew over it. It never awoke, thus beginning the Sleeping Bear Dunes. People trek for miles across these dunes to see the beautiful waters, few knowing what may slumber beneath.

Another legend tells of a woman of noble birth taking her place under a great assembly of the hosts of heaven above. A cloud of witnesses treks across the celestial sky to see her splendor, fully aware of the great mystery she holds. Only, in the legend, the woman too is asleep. She does not know the full power and beauty that encompass her. That she is now a part of.

No one knows why she fell asleep beside the eternal waters. But a world that whispers of her beauty and stops to stare at her transcendent majesty wonders if she will awaken. It hopes the legend is true and there really is a deeply profound mystery buried beneath.

She is the church.

It's time for her to awaken to the sound of rushing waters and the brightness of the noonday sun. Like her Savior, it is her splendor the world is waiting to see, that of a spotless bride radiant in glory. But she must rise up uncovered by sands the years of wind have carried over her. She must stir again and awaken.

And whose call is it to stir her?

There is an elect who God has chosen to do it. It isn't a pastor alone. This particular time, it is not women. This job God has appointed to *every man*.

They are the ones God has destined, long before time, to raise up torches and glass jars and blow their trumpets. They are the ones whose silence up until now, as they marched around the city, was for only this moment to roar. They are the ones to rush into the snowy den, slay a tiger, and emerge undaunted by armies.

To freeze a hand to the hilt of a sword.

To be mighty men.

God calls every man to be a leader. This is a call every man *must* answer. The church, God's sleeping beauty, rests before him. He must awaken her.

Take this call, and the church will fall into place behind him. Answer it, and the world cannot stop them with her by his side.

Men have searched for mission in the long hours beating the territory on the work trail, chiseling the pounds on the treadmill. My best friend, Luke, looked in the mirror months ago and didn't see the hulking warrior he'd always been. The reflection disappointed him. In a moment, something snapped he would never consider in the Greek godhood of our twenties. He began the dreaded...cardio. One look in the mirror and now nothing can stop him from tearing up the gym. This time the one with headbands as well as powdered barbells.

What is keeping us from accepting the one great mission of our lives? In a moment, we will all be changed and taken up with Christ. Perhaps it's time we look in the mirror. What else could possibly be worth living for in the meantime than this?

THE SEARCH

We've been hard-wired for a mission. When our hands aren't freezing to swords, they're searching for equivalents. One evening a few months ago, I celebrated the Jewish Passover, with explanations of how the symbolism points to Christ. At my favorite part of the ceremony, we ate horseradish on unleavened bread, which represent the suffering and haste of the Israelites.

As usual, I shoveled loads of horseradish onto a thin piece of flat bread to maximize my suffering. Not to be outdone, Mike, the friend next to me, built a small fortress of horseradish and experimented with the possible shades of red in the human face. Pretty soon we were feverishly loading pallets of suffering onto our plates, relishing the challenge to our toughness.

Mike leaned in, quipping, "I've done so many things to cause myself pain; it's nice to do it for a good reason for once."

We thrive on challenge as men. Isn't it time we glorify God with this drive? Isn't it time we channel it for the one mission we were created for?

I should add—purposely hurting oneself doesn't glorify God. But this was a way to enjoy God while remembering the Israelites' pain. Coincidentally, the fun ended when I yelled out, "Pass the suffering. My wife hasn't had enough!"

I admit it was ill-timed, since she was in her third trimester with our son.

But in a word, what keeps us from taking the challenge before us and our legitimate place as men leading the church? What prevents us from awakening the sleeping beauty?

Passivity.

The book *Raising a Modern Day Knight* teaches four pillars of being a man. At an early age, they became legendary in our family. My dad taught us the four pillars as a warrior's code. They were pivotal in our development as men. The pillars are:

1. Rejecting Passivity

2. Accepting Responsibility
3. Leading Courageously
4. Expecting the Greater Reward (God's Reward)

I remember one time my dad took me to a men's breakfast at church as a young boy. I was in awe of these great heroes of our church. At the beginning of the talk, the speaker asked what it is to be a man. He waited. Dad turned to me and said, "John-Peter, you know. Stand up and tell them." I hopped out of my seat and rattled them off, "Reject passivity, accept responsibility, lead courageously, and expect the great reward, God's reward!" The men looked at me for a moment, dumbfounded.

The training stuck. All four of us can still recite them to this day.

And though these four principles mark a godly man, many never get beyond the passivity part. Truth be told, I've often found myself tripping up on it. All the rest go down like dominoes.

Before we fully understood our nature, we could get by with remaining uninvolved and absent from the mission. There were pastors and better men for that. But now we know God designed us as more than passive participants. We aren't invited to a pew to be a notch on the church head count. It isn't enough to let the pastor be the guy or our wives pick up the slack. Our call is unmistakable. It resounds through God's Word.

We are pastors.

The stakes couldn't be higher. The Bride slumbers at our feet under layers of sand the world has dumped on her.

And we are called to save her.

In *A Day at the Races,* one of the Marx Brothers, Groucho, masquerades as a doctor to a particularly rich patient, although he's really a horse doctor. The hospital is in danger of closing its doors, and, despite his lack of credentials, his presence there matters. When confronted with his deception by an employee played by Chico Marx, Groucho snatches his hat and bag and heads for the door. Attempting to convince him to stay, Chico asks if he's a man or a mouse. Groucho responds, "Put a piece of cheese down there and you'll find out."

God has made us men. The awesome ramifications of this should rock us.

Men who are fed up with sitting in the pew dreaming of Sunday afternoon football, whose hearts yearn for a mission beyond the next promotion or upgrade to their front landscape, who hear the quiet cry within to lead, take risks, and use their God-given desires for *something more*, should be impacted that they matter.

God designed us for a purpose. He wrote it in the heavens. He wrote it on our hearts. It is the destiny of our lives. Now, all we have to do is take the fleeting moments of our lives and stand up and do something. Our pulpits are all around us. Our congregants, though they may be few, are at our feet. And God won't allow our position to be taken by anyone else.

Sure, if we prefer passivity, we can go back to bets on who will score more points on Sunday Night Football. And it will continue long after we're gone without a hint of difference. But we know we were made for something more.

And once a man knows who he is, he's a dangerous thing.

We've been called. God has made us pastors. The Bride, his sleeping beauty, quietly stirs, waiting to be awakened. She can be transformed into glory, "without spot or blemish," she only needs to be led. And the job is ours.

It's time for us to pastor her.

Now all we need is a study Bible. Or a piece of cheese.

PREPARING HIS HEART

My dad often tells the story of a college friend who had an unusual perspective on the sword of the Spirit, the Word of

God. "While it is the offensive weapon of the armor of God," he would say, sliding his hand as a dagger toward his heart, "its primary purpose is to turn around and use on us."

Hebrews 4:12 says, "For the word of God is living and active. Sharper than any double-edged sword, it penetrates even to dividing soul and spirit, joints and marrow; it judges the thoughts and attitudes of the heart."

The Word is a mighty weapon. It has "divine power to demolish strongholds" (2 Cor. 10:4). It is used to "demolish arguments and every pretension that sets itself up against the knowledge of God" (v.5). It has authority over demons and principalities. But its most important purpose is it to cut away sin in our lives.

Like my dad's college friend, we must turn the "dagger" of the Spirit on ourselves to trim our own hearts. It divides between wisdom and foolishness, righteousness and sin, truth and lie. It teaches and convicts.

There is much to this.

As pastors, men cannot lead their families and churches in ways they are not yet mature. And if men are pastors, they need to start thinking of themselves as pastors and studying the Word like one.

So it's time to bulk up.

BECOMING A CHAMPIONSHIP COACH

When I was in high school, I used to pray every day God would make me "bigger and stronger." He did, and that was a good thing. But eternal manhood is becoming bigger and stronger in God and "has value for all things" (1 Tim. 4:8).

It's time to build our spiritual muscles.
And like Rocky in the *Rocky* movie series, we need Mick, a trainer, who can train us to win the fight.

That's discipleship. The first step to becoming a wise leader is learning from a wiser one. The apostles had Jesus. It's important a man have a mentor.

My dad is that to me. He has trained me to be a man of God from childhood. When I encounter difficulties, I go to him even now. He gives wise, straight advice about the right course.

However, a man has a responsibility not to simply accept advice, even from wise men, but to judge it. At times my dad suggests something I know deep down isn't the best decision. He may not have all the facts; I may recognize a better option. But that's the point. One balances one's opinions with wiser men, then judges personally what to do. If a man thoughtlessly accepts advice, he will never become a strong leader.

But he must seek out wise men to coach him.

Interestingly, after wrestling for almost a decade and seeing many programs, I've observed most high school wrestling coaches are pretty much the same. They coach the way they were coached and know little else. Usually, they've picked up a few strengths but are rather poor coaches. Few reach beyond themselves to become better.

My dad modeled a different approach for me. When he learned he would take over my high school wrestling team after I graduated, he sought out the coach of one of the two best high school teams in the nation. At the NCAA wrestling tournament, he spent three days picking the accomplished coach's brain on how to run a championship program. Honestly, Dad would talk wrestling anywhere to glean ideas.

He did, indeed, take over the team the next year, a huge project with a 1-9 previous record. His first year we were 8-8. The next, we switched to the best tournaments in the area and finished 19-6, with our entire JV line-up competing against the previous year's schedule. We never told the schools on the original schedule they were wrestling our JV team.

The third year we won 1st place at seven tournaments, including the coveted area tournament, beating a team annually ranked among the best in the state. That team is currently #16 in the nation.

I'd like to say we were able to achieve all this because my dad is such a talented guy. Really, he was a visionary. He learned from the best and spent significant time forming his leadership after theirs. Those he saw consistently at the top, he followed. And he talked wrestling everywhere.

If we are serious about pastoring our homes and, in some measure, the church, men need to do the same—seek out the best and learn from them. We need to talk God everywhere.

Really, we need to be hungry to disciple the best family possible in Christ, just like my dad was hungry to coach the best team possible.

If we have this perspective, which is the call, we will not fail.

God promises in the Word.

"Plans fail for lack of counsel, but with many advisors they succeed" (Prov. 15:22).

Often, we are haphazard about our "team," and when we coach we just pass along the way we were coached. And if we didn't grow up on a championship team, that doesn't produce results. But if we take the time to study the best, we will build our families into perennial powers.

In addition, we need other guys with whom we can regularly discuss our families. I have men I trust to share my struggles, ideas from the Word, and plans and passions to carry them out. We've created a culture of hunger for God. Their hearts light mine on fire.

That is an environment in which a man can succeed as the leader God wants him to be.

Avoiding deep discussions, rarely bringing up God with friends, and not seeking wise counsel create a culture of leading by accident. Of pastoring on auto-pilot. And like most coaches, it doesn't produce winning teams.

In church recently, the pastor asked, "If you aren't willing to get serious with God for your own life, might I suggest you do it for your children?"

I don't know a man who wouldn't love to coach a winning team.

We have one. It is ours to form, strategize, train, and lead. We can brainstorm and build it from the ground up. We already have the head coaching job. We just have to dream. Let's get our heads together and build a program fit for the championships.

GROWING LIKE WEEDS

The Bible uses the analogy of fields ripe for a harvest. In our own lives, they are ripest where we control the flow of water, the fertilizer, and the nutrients in the soil. They are ripest where we can make the conditions as rich as possible—in our homes.

But, first, to be a good pastor, a man must cultivate his own soil. His primary duty is his relationship with God.

A pastor's relationship with God is in danger if his only weekly Bible study is to prepare for his sermon on Sunday. Likewise, God desires we spend regular time with him in his Word. Just to be with him.

To grow. To hear him speak. To hear him *love us*. To love him.

Far more important than anything we could accomplish is being with God—worshiping and enjoying him.

A year or so ago, my mom received an epiphany from God. She said it occurred to her, "The purpose in life is to love God and to let him love us."

It doesn't get simpler or hit closer to the heart of the matter than that.

Volumes could be written about our difficulty to let God love us. To accept in our hearts without insecurity how much he cherishes everything about us. It's hard to do. But we aren't meant to struggle through life alone; there is a Lover of our souls. Many could be written about slowing down our frantic pace to enjoy and love God, as well.

So the pastor's first duty is to prepare his heart. He prepares it for God. As an altar of love and worship. But as he does, he also prepares it for ministry.

My dad's best friend, Roger, bought a home a few years ago and hired a company to fertilize the landscape. The neighborhood lavishly watered all the properties with its own sprinkler system. What Roger didn't know, and what makes this story interesting, was they also fertilized. With a double portion of fertilizer and a healthy supply of water, those bushes leapt up in size. After a short time, they dwarfed the other plants in the neighborhood.

Soon Roger had to have someone trim the tops of the bushes inside his fence because they'd formed a solid wall, risen above the fence, and climbed into the neighbor's yard. They'd become mutant shrubbery.

In a way, God wants us to be mutant shrubs like those plants. He wants us to soak in the ideal environment of sun, limitless water, and a double portion of his fertilizer. He wants our roots to grow so deep in him we could weather anything, until we rise above the fences like towers.

To paraphrase Isaiah 61, God has sent the Holy Spirit in abundance to heal, free, and prosper. He says he'll give us "a double portion" (v.7) and "[we] will be called oaks of righteousness, the planting of the Lord, that he may be glorified" (v.3). This will happen "as the soil makes the sprout come up and a garden causes seeds to grow" (v.11).

This is God's analogy.

Oaks are very large trees. They have vast root systems.

Roger watered and lavishly fertilized his plants and they grew to the heavens.

God wants us to soak up his limitless love, Word, and Holy Spirit and grow like oaks the same way. To the heavens.

"The Spirit and the bride say, 'Come!' And let him who hears say, 'Come!' Whoever is thirsty, let him come; and whoever wishes, let him take the water of life without price" (Rev. 22:17).

On your list of priorities, God puts having this type of relationship with him at the top. Do you not get a little excited?

So your first job as a pastor is to prepare your heart for God. To get in the Word daily. To worship daily. To enjoy and love him. In rich, real relationship.

A DOUBLE PORTION

I've spoken about my father's journey as a wrestling coach. I should relay his faith journey, as well.

When he came to Christ, as most of us, Dad knew he needed a crash course in a different mindset than he'd learned. A member of a large Christian organization, he had scores of training tapes at his disposal. He was a college student with time on his hands, so he spent an hour reading his Bible and another hour worshiping and praying every day. And he soaked his mind in those tapes, listening to two or three a night.

A double portion of fertilizer and water.

One can grow a lot from that kind of immersion.

Barry McGuire was a popular singer in the 1960's. His hit song, "Eve of Destruction," reached number one on the charts. He eventually gave his life to Christ, and on one of his live albums, he mentions a conversation that followed with one of his friends. His friend complained about the Christian songs he'd begun to sing, accusing, "You're brainwashed!" Barry responded, "Man, my brain needed a good washing."

Like Barry, my dad knew his brain needed a good washing. Every man's does.

That's why the Bible isn't meant to be read once and set aside because we know it already. We have to keep washing with the water of the Word all our lives. You wouldn't stop showering since you showered once last week, would you? After a few days, your wife might notice.

Nor would you quit feeding a plant because you watered and fertilized it heavily one week last month.

An hour a day reading the Bible. An hour worshiping and praying. Two or three teaching tapes a night.

That's one mutant shrubbery.

You might not have that much time (though many spend quite a lot in front of the TV), but there are ways to be creative. My brother Richard used to listen to the Bible on CD as he walked to class in high school. My dad and I built a deck listening to the entire gospel of Mark. That was an experience I'll never forget. A band of us in college even carried pocket Bibles everywhere for split-second sparring. There are no rules for growth. And seriously, if there were rules about fertilizing, Roger probably broke them. But, like his plants, we need to be saturated.

Years after my dad's initial immersion of discipleship passed, it has translated into a steady stream. He reads his Bible every morning. When I was born, he started reading it each year. He switched to every two for a while; now he's back to one. Since then he's read the Bible 28 times. Like Roger's lawn, he continues a constant flow to his soul to keep it thick, lush, and green.

His roots are deep in God.

He also takes 20 minutes to worship God every day, singing songs and speaking praises of love. He began this with our family when I could do little more than rap on a drum.

Taking daily worship time with God was invaluable training from an early age to regularly "water our gardens." We grew up with a close, real relationship with God.

I think of a luxuriant wall of plants, towering over the fences and reaching into the neighbor's yard. I think of innumerable tapes, hours of study, family prayer times, and the steady sprinkling of a Bible that has been read 28 times.

When you are growing, you are ready to give.

When your roots have sunk deep in God, your maturity in Christ and wisdom tower as an oak of righteousness.

And when you have been discipled by the best and lead with a band of brothers hungry for God, you are ready to pastor.

Chapter Nine

LOCKED IN LITTLE TREASURE CHESTS

Listening and Assessing…

A *great* date, I thought. Both of us had been pretty quiet. The idea to take the family out for ice cream on date night now seemed like not such a good idea.

It isn't like *nothing* had happened, though. Angela had hovered with eagle-eye precision over Luke's stroller at every whimper.

And I...I had felt a little neglected, to say the least.

But all was not against us. The setting was serene. An ocean breeze whisked off the glistening waters as waves rushed up the shore, pouring their churning contents over the cool white sand as dusk approached. Munching the last bits of waffle cone filled with delicious ice cream from our favorite parlor by the beach, we found ourselves at an ideal spot to be swept away.

Yet, as the stroller bumped and rattled over the brick paver surrounding the park, I grew more frustrated.

It's not as though I hadn't tried.

I'd made a few half-hearted swipes at her hand, once securing it for a total of twenty seconds. Before a gasp from Luke pulled it away.

Even here, the prospect of romance appeared bleak.

However, one redeeming moment survived the date.

At the top of the hill in the park, I released Luke's stroller and it picked up speed, careening down the sidewalk, until the absolute last second when I swooped in and snatched it before sidewalk met grass in an abrupt conclusion.

At the end of the night, when we returned home and were finally alone, Angela told me she'd felt distant from me all day.

Really? Distant from me?

I guess there's something I'd been missing.

THE DREAMS OF A CHILD

The first duty of a man to his congregation is not sexy. It's not like date night. Not even date night out with the family for ice cream (which is *not* date night). It is, however, surprisingly obvious. It's listening.

If a pastor's job is to grow his congregation, he cannot do so unless he knows its condition. That's why listening is so important.

For the pastor of a home, it helps to recognize God's plan for his family. Each person is unique, with his or her own personality, interests, dreams, and hopes. And each is important to God.

When a baby is in its mother's womb, it's safe and warm. It hovers in a liquid sack, receives food and water, and is surrounded by its mother. Its little baby dreams begin to form, each a seed soon to sprout into a specific part of God's plan for mankind. I imagine all it wants is to be loved, to be completely accepted and cherished by Mommy and Daddy.

I think of this perspective when I meet adults. Each one entered the world completely vulnerable and with the most innocent heart and dreams. Each just wanted to be loved.

From that perspective of sensitivity I minister.

Those dreams were so little and fragile when they were born. That personality so tender and impressionable. It makes me weep to think what the world has done to so many helpless babies' personalities and dreams, hardened as they become men and women.

That's where your job comes in. The job of a pastor is to restore that heart. To heal.

It is the hearts and minds of those in his care he specializes in. As Colossians says, "We proclaim him, admonishing and teaching everyone with all wisdom, so that we may present everyone perfect in Christ" (Col. 1:28).

That's the goal. To present them perfect in Christ.

To do that, one must listen.

LOCKED IN LITTLE TREASURE CHESTS

I love coming home to my wife after a long day. There's nothing better than having her look up at me from the couch and smile. Sometimes, though, she'll look a little...different. Her smile will only turn up at one corner of her mouth. The usually chipper greeting will be a quiet, "Hey." It's not hard to notice something is wrong.

It could be anything, as most men know, from a text she sent that I didn't read, to a hard day at work.

What is important is that I recognize it. It's also vitally important I recognize what emotion is behind what she's feeling.

Oh, we practice expressing our feelings. We tell each other what we need and how we feel. Still, on a deeper level, it's my job to watch the overall care of her soul. Rarely will she come to me and say, "These are my deepest wounds. I need you to help heal me."

But that is a crucial part of making her perfect in Christ.

So a man must listen very carefully. She will reveal the ways she needs him to lead her.

The goal is to identify the lie she believes and replace it with the truth.

To do that, I'm going to draw upon an unlikely source: psychology. Now don't freak out. This isn't going to be ultra-academic or mind-bogglingly intellectual. It's actually going to be quite simple.

A man needs to understand the way people think and the beliefs they develop about themselves. It's also helpful to learn family dynamics and the roles people take in families. Knowing how people think can help you recognize the clues to what your family members believe that may hurt them.

When I was getting to know a friend, Kim, I noticed a lack of confidence in certain areas of her life. Overall a confident and assertive woman, she seemed uncertain about aspects of her personality. Her sister, on the other hand, was extremely confident in those same areas. Kim was introverted, but her sister was the consummate extrovert.

Laughing over old times, a clue to the dynamic behind her insecurity was revealed in a harmless childhood story. Years before, Kim's teacher had called her parents. Kim always drew normal, pretty pictures of rainbows and sunny skies. Everything a child finds fascinating. Then one day, the drawings changed. She started drawing pictures of her family in all black. When the teacher asked her about it, Kim cried saying, "Mommy and Daddy love my sister and don't love me."

I was heart-broken when I heard this story. I understood it.

She had received the message from her mom and dad that they didn't love her. I happen to know her parents. They are wonderful parents who absolutely adore their kids and show it every chance they get. But in this instance, that wasn't enough. All that mattered was what *she believed*.

And I saw the clue was in the relationship dynamic. Kim's sister made a show wherever she went and people loved it. She was always vying for attention. Therefore, she received more and more confidence from their affirmation. Little Kimmie, a beautiful, introverted girl with a sensitive heart, ruminated over her needs but rarely expressed them. Her parents showed her love. But her sister required so much attention that at times she unknowingly diverted it from Kim.

That's why Kim drew in black. She received the message somewhere in the bustle of family life at home that she wasn't as loved as her sister. Also, for some reason, when friends or relatives gave them dolls or toys, they unwittingly chose the pink for her sister and the blue for Kim. She shared with me once, without bitterness, how it upset her she was always given the boy color. She used to ask herself, *why couldn't she ever get the pink?* Of course, she wouldn't say a thing. And locked inside a little treasure chest are all these pieces. Put them together and you can imagine what messages might sink into a little girl's heart. They break mine.

Understanding how people think and the clues from their past can help explain their hurts now. Listening and recognizing them allows us to unlock these mysteries and heal with the truth.

And that is the state of the world. Broken people with little pieces locked inside treasure chests. All hoping someday they will meet someone with the key. To make sense of it all.

I love the human heart. It is such a beautiful, fragile thing. Pastoring cares for it, as "a hen gathers her chicks under her wings" (Luke 13:34). It says nothing's going to touch you. God is here.

I am fiercely passionate about seeing hearts set free by believing the truth that the wound told them they could never believe. "You will know the truth, and the truth will set you free" (John 8:32).

It's time we learn the truth.

Truth is not what we feel or think. It is what God says, because, quite simply, it is what is. While the earth, emotions, and experience give way around us, it is a city that will not fall. When the whole world washes away, it is a rock. In the face of life's pain and injustice, its faithfulness never fails. It produces a heart fully alive and free. Though it lives in the world, it soars in spite of it.

Truth is little pieces locked in treasure chests gingerly taken into the light to be made whole.

At the heart of it is every little baby's dream—that we are unfathomably accepted and loved. And we always will be.

I have discovered our deepest dreams, the ones we can't believe yet desperately wish were true, are usually what is *most* true in our lives. Like the foreshadowing of a great story in the human heart, the stolen parts are the most valuable. They will be restored; the climax is a few pages away. Rest easy, it has already been written.

God has the key to these mysteries, and he will teach us if we will listen.

DEMYSTIFYING THE THEFT

Kim's example is classic and common. The more we observe people, the more we intuitively see patterns in these mysteries. And the more we can understand and minister to them.

I strongly recommend studying people. Study your Bible more, so you know truth. But get to know people, too. And those principles that reveal how God made us think and interact let transform your ministry.

Kim and her parents laugh about the black drawings today. They're in the past; everyone is confident of each other's love. But my heart still goes out to little Kimmie and those like her. The insecurities that relate to those early messages often remain. The truth is most of us have them.

No matter how amazing one's parents or how great one's life, harmful messages can get through. Satan's goal is to "steal and kill and destroy" (John 10:10). I've found stealing, killing, and destroying isn't some phantom spiritual potion or mystical attack, but rather, a practical siege over one's thoughts. Traumatic experiences leave an imprint, and we struggle to cope with our new reality of the world.

The battle is over beliefs. Believe the truth and we are safe, healthy, fine. Believe the lie and the thief of our flesh tries to steal, kill, and destroy what is central to our hearts.

But there's no reason to fear. Really, knowing should be a relief. There is an enemy. He is defeated by the cross. So he wages war in the mind, trying to spoil our joy when he can. It isn't as spooky as we have imagined. The tragedy, the theft, is if he can make us disbelieve who we are, he can make life feel like a loss. But he can't change what is true about our lives one bit, only our attitude or perception of it.

My dad calls this smoke and mirrors. They are scare tactics and lies. It's hard to accept the truth when we *feel* something so strongly. But when we know his plan, we've already won. Paul says, "We are not ignorant of his schemes" (2 Cor. 2:11).

And you should not be ignorant of them in your family.

WASHING WITH THE WORD

You hear a hurt surface or see a gradual attitude change in your wife. Ask about it. Listen to her heart, not just what she says. Encourage there.

Usually, doubts begin at what is most valuable in a person's heart. And what is most true. That should be a confirmation of God's special mission there. Wrapped in the fragile vulnerability of a desire of the heart is its special worth to God. The lie targets God's most intimate design about a person. It often confirms the opposite of the attack is true—it is the place God's heart is most deeply involved.

Your ministry is to apply the healing balm of the Word of God and what it says about your family right at the places they need it most. Whether they recognize it or not, you recognize it.

Can you see how important it is for you to know God's Word? Can you see how important it is, as the family pastor, to be mature and wise in Christ?

And to be listening?

It is as important as the hearts of the people you love most.

Listen to their passions. Listen to their hearts. What stirs in their love for God? Never lose sight of your family's former passions and current progress in him. If their desires grow cold, they lose confidence in themselves or are drawn in by the allure of the world, it is your job to recognize whether the root is from hopelessness, depression, insecurity, or any other quiet lie. The Lord will give you, as pastor, insight into this.

That is where a man reinforces with the truth. That is where he loves.

If a man keeps personal tabs on his wife's and children's spiritual lives, thoughts, and emotions, he will make an immeasurable impact in establishing the kingdom of God in the hearts that desperately need it.

That is your responsibility. "So that we may present everyone perfect in Christ" (Col. 1:28).

Perfection does not mean being without sin, but rather reaching completion—maturity.

To help his family reach maturity, a man needs to hear them.

What does my wife believe? The sighs I see and frustrations I know she's going through, do they represent lies struggling with her heart? How can I encourage and re-inspire her?

When I minister to Angela, I check her response. Do her eyes tell me she believes what I am saying about her? If not, I know the message hasn't gotten through yet.

Your mission isn't accomplished when you've said the truth. It's accomplished when she believes it.

Like my dad's brain, our wives and children need washing, often many times until completely clean.

"Washing with water through the Word" (Eph. 5:26).

That's the job. And I bet you already know where many of the wounds lie.

But the dirt doesn't usually come off the first time. My dad tells my mom, "I love you," at least seven times a day in various ways. So I try to do the same. Angela knows it well, but how much she needs to hear it. Imagine everything she may not yet believe and how many times she needs to hear of those: her beauty, her worth, her personality, her job as a wife and mother, her body, her gifts, her value to me and the family. The list goes on for every woman. And every child. So many treasures are buried under years of rubble, but "Behold," in the midst of it…"I make all things new" (Rev. 21:5, KJV).

Remember, your wife's wounds were probably reinforced many, many times. In those areas, her brain needs rinsing with the gentle, refreshing Word of God over and over until the lies have been washed away. Until she finally believes.

Oh, she'll give hints when she doesn't yet. She'll sigh, half roll her eyes. Angela responds with a sheepish, "Thanks," if she doesn't totally receive my compliment of her beauty. So I reinforce.

There's a point at which a woman gives up and finally believes what you say about her is true. Usually she'll first concede she knows *you* feel that way about her. But that's not the finish line; it is only a rest stop. She doesn't yet embrace it herself. The end goal is when she believes what God sees in her. It is the breaking of the tape, when she recognizes her true value, free of "spot or blemish." That's a moment worth raising one's arms in victory.

Our families, as our congregations, constantly give us clues to what they need. It's time we read them. It's time we observe the body language, interpret the emotion in the eyes. Parents quickly recognize a baby's cries and whether the child is hungry, tired, or annoyed; we should be able to read the signs as they grow a few years older, as well.

THE SIGNS

Part of this is noticing family dynamics—the roles family members take—and anticipating how that will affect them in the future. We need to see the patterns and pitfalls ahead.

Healthy family dynamics are essential for healthy, mature lives. When men understand how people think and what causes negative messages, they can set healthy patterns to protect their family's hearts and minds for years to come.

And recognizing the messages that form can be incredibly practical. Yet priceless.

Watch anyone's eyes and you will read volumes there.

Start with looking for "love, joy, peace, patience, kindness, goodness, faithfulness, gentleness, and self-control" (Gal. 5:22-23).

Those are the fruit of the Spirit. They're the fruit of a life matured in God. They are the well-spring flowing up from a person's heart.

The Bible says, "Guard your heart, for it is the well-spring of eternal life" (Prov. 4:23), and "The eye is the lamp of the body" (Matt. 6:22).

Look deeply in those eyes. Encourage the fruit of the Spirit you see reflected there, growing in their hearts. Guard it. It is precious. If there is fruit of the flesh, you'll find it there, too. Whether good or bad, you'll see it in their eyes. You'll also see it in their lives, but you have to be paying attention. Often the clues are small, but big matters of the heart lie behind them. The seeds may be easy to excuse or dismiss. Only years later will you see them produced in full, ripe fruit. People wonder then how their children got so far, but it's the simple product of what was planted and cultivated in their hearts.

If you find interpreting your family's emotional and spiritual state difficult, there's an easy place to start: ask. Honest questions can go a long way in understanding someone. Ask until you are confident of the answers.

God has made you an overseer. He wants you to see.

There is little in life more satisfying than being deeply understood and appreciated by another person. Listen and hear your wife's and children's hearts. Love them there.

And your family, your flock, will be truly grateful to have you as a leader.

-Chapter Ten-
THE TEAM COACH

ᴧ

Discipling…

We crouched around the mat as seconds ticked off the clock, everyone thinking we could—we *might*—do the unthinkable.

Canton Wrestling hadn't beaten its cross-town rival, Salem, in twelve years. Those weren't twelve years of friendly close calls, either. It was over a decade of dominance—bitter, in your face, taunting dominance.

In the previous Canton coach's last year, during a usual spat, he swore to the Salem coach he would beat them. They lost 48-9.

Enter Dad & Co. He brought in top assistants, a new work ethic, and a visionary approach to leadership and began rebuilding the rubble that was Canton Wrestling from ground zero.

And here we found ourselves, three years later, on the verge of the unthinkable—beating Salem for the first time since anyone could remember.

They were no pushovers, either. Multiple wrestlers who would compete at the state tournament, the same hard-nosed, downright mean coaching staff; they were the same old Salem.

Only, we were not the same.

So it was pure joy when our 145 pounder turned to the bench, flexing in ecstatic disbelief after pinning his wrestler.

And when our heavyweight arose with the same look in his eyes, we had finally done it. We had defeated the giant. We had beaten Salem.

One of the coaches and I leapt and embraced mid-flight, months of hard work released in the simple pleasure of two men realizing they'd shocked the world. Behind us, a whole team of wrestlers—teammates, friends, and brothers—did the same.

It is one of the most indelible memories of my coaching career.

If you want the same experience for your family, one thing must precede it—vision.

As I've said, Dad was a visionary for our team. He saw exactly where we were going. He knew how to get there; he showed us the way. Sure enough, to everyone's surprise but him, we reached it.

And, let me tell you, there's no sweeter feeling than walking back to the team bench after shaking hands with a freshly defeated foe.

THE TASK OF A LEADER

A great leader has a vision for his organization. He inspires and empowers the people around him to accomplish it.

The same is true in the family.

Two years ago, my new fiancé, Angela, and I listened to a popular family podcast, months before she would become my wife. It was one of our favorite after-dinner activities to sit and listen in preparation for marriage.

In the evening's particular broadcast, the podcasters were discussing men's and women's roles. They explained the directions: men love your wives, women respect your husbands. Then they read an email from a woman who complained her husband kept telling her she needed to submit. Here's the kicker—the speakers responded by pointing out to their listeners that the specific part of the passage about submitting was not written to the husband. He was only supposed to read his part. The part to his wife was not his business.

I was shocked to hear this advice. It couldn't have been more wrong. It completely missed the intent of their natures. If the man is the leader in Christ, isn't he ultimately responsible for all?

The head football coach doesn't directly oversee the defense. The defensive coordinator does. The head coach entrusts responsibility to him and empowers him to do his job. But he ultimately answers for how he leads his assistants in handling each part of the team.

Put another way, someone once told me the husband's job is to lead; it isn't his business whether his wife follows. But that's missing the point of good leadership. I wouldn't consider a coach a good coach if he instructed the team to begin practice and then shrugged when everyone walked off. He wouldn't throw up his hands and say, "Oh, well I did my job. I led. It's not my business whether they follow." How he leads in response to that experience defines his leadership of the team, as well as his wisdom.

The truth is the husband's job *is* to disciple his wife. That's what a biblical leader does. He isn't aggressive or demanding. He lovingly, gently teaches her from the Word.

The problem was not in what the husband from the email said. It is his responsibility to teach his wife. The problem appears to be in *how* he said it. Throwing his weight around or being harsh isn't going to inspire anyone. This matter especially requires gentleness, patience, and love. But a husband should always point his wife, as well as his children, to the Word of God.

I wrote the chapter on preparing a man's heart, in part, because a man needs to be humble to be a good leader. He must notice the log in his own eye quicker than the speck in another's. A successful leader empowers his wife to do her job, trusts her to do it, and honors her richly for her work. One who walks all over his wife hurts the person most important to him. As a leader, he cripples his "team" by not treating her with respect. He's forgotten his first instruction to love and his family will never be a success until he gets it right.

However, a man may not give up his role in a misguided attempt to empower. True empowering does so *with* leadership, not by relinquishing it. God has given man this responsibility, as he gave the servant in Luke a mina. Only a wicked one would bury it in the ground.

Leading, taking responsibility for the *whole* team, is his job.

Every now and then I come across a Christian woman whose behavior is clearly out of order, and I wonder how her husband can put up with it. I know it's not possible for him to ignore how she lashes out at people or maliciously gossips. Most likely, he's cowered into a corner and accepted it. He has given up his role. And look at the results it's produced. He's lost the team. It is undisciplined and disorganized—no good comes of it; it never wins games. They probably have some sort of habitual compromise in which he has authority in name, a paper leader, but she has bull-dozed all control in her rebellious areas and he won't put up a fight.

It's important to note, although she will answer to God for everything she's done, *so will he.* It's his responsibility to disciple his wife in living like Christ. That is a man's job. Is it so surprising authority has a purpose? A general maintains order in the ranks and a level of conduct and discipline among his officers. A coach passes on to his assistants his philosophies and leadership style. And a husband, with love and respect, shepherds his wife and kids.

"Admonishing and teaching with all wisdom so that he may present everyone perfect in Christ."

"Cleansing her by the washing with water through the Word...to present her to himself as a radiant church, without stain or wrinkle or any other blemish, but holy and blameless."

Do you notice the similarities? The first refers to pastors; the second to husbands. Both lovingly disciple to bring to perfection in Christ.

This truth seems lost on modern culture. They know man is the head of the family, but they don't understand what that looks like. It's an ambiguous job title that sounds nice but lacks weight. But his leadership is extremely clear and surprisingly practical.

The job of the pastor is to care for the hearts and minds of the people, to teach and disciple. That's the job of the husband, too. Same design of masculinity. Same purpose.

However, the practical workings of this are rarely taught. They are more than making final decisions. The husband is called to lead, provide vision, and disciple.

How else can he present her to himself without spot or blemish? By having the final say on who should work and where the kids will go to school? A man's purpose in Ephesians is to cleanse his wife with the Word and to present her to himself in all her glory. Just like Jesus does for the church. And the defining characteristic of this is love.

Isn't it beautiful?

But if he isn't willing to lead it all falls apart.

TAKING THE LEAD

God gave my mom a prophecy once that without knowledge the people perish. She looked it up and found, "Where there is no vision, the people perish, but happy is he who keeps the law" (Prov. 29:18, KJV/NKJV).

The knowledge people need is of the Lord's ways and his leading. Without vision of where they are going, God's people languish with no clear purpose and stray. If they have it, they fulfill his plan for them with joy. The vision directs them to the path.

For a godly man, the vision is how he sees the Lord leading his family to maturity in Christ.

He trains and leads them according to that vision.

The extent of this is as broad as the areas of Christian living: communication, dealing with conflict, finances, forgiveness, gifts of the Spirit, faith, having a proper attitude, being disciplined, perseverance, and seeing God's perspective on suffering. The list goes on and on. In whatever areas need growth, a man lovingly teaches.

Few couples seem to understand this. Countless guys compromise on issues they feel are important because they don't want to tread on their wives' toes or they wish to be a team player. In matters of sacrifice, I respect that. Guys who flip down the toilet seat and pick up a magazine to pee have my admiration. There will be no lowering of lid by a woman in their houses. That's a matter to compromise.

But when doctrinal issues or family direction is at stake, a man must not compromise. He listens to his wife and considers her opinions and advice carefully. But if his conscience doesn't allow him to change, he may never cave in the name of sacrifice. God gave the guidance of the family to him as his responsibility.

Compromise in everything you can to put her first, but never on the vision. Don't give up where you see God leading your family. That isn't love. It will only damage your family in the long run. Many marriages have suffered from this.

However, no man is right all the time. Mistakes will be made, so listening carefully to your wife is crucial. Asking forgiveness is, too.

When Angela and I were preparing for marriage, both of us were uncertain how this would work out. It was hard for her to accept adapting in certain areas, and it was hard for me to courageously set the direction I saw God leading, while not compromising truth. What helped was we both knew each was fully committed to growing in God. I knew she was submitted to God's Word and willing to change to it, and she knew the same was true of me.

And an amazing thing happened.

The more we communicated and the more we studied, the more we came to agreement in the Word.

THE TEAM IDENTITY: TEAM 134

A few times in fights when we were recently married, I gently said to my wife, "That's not what Demsicks do. This is how we respond..." and then I showed her. I could have used the word "Christians," but there's specific importance when referring to the family vision. There's a set of values, attitudes, behaviors, and beliefs to being Christian based on the Word of God. They are not open to choice. There's right and wrong. Mature and immature. Those God has illumined to me, I pass on in what it means to be "Demsick."

This is no different from great leadership on a sports team or in a company. The leader catches a vision, studies it, and learns from others how to achieve the vision. He passes the specific vision on to his team. He uses the team identity to bring them together in the face of the mission. They love the university or company they represent. They identify with it and relish it. But they also take great identity from the specific team.

The University of Michigan football team has a tradition that highlights this. They refer to each team by the number of years since the program's inception. This year is Team 134. To start every meeting, the head coach says, "Team...," to which the players respond, "134!" "Win..." "Big Ten!" "Beat..." "Ohio!" They are all Michigan. But they are also Team 134. And the identity draws them together.

It focuses them on the vision and empowers them to be successful in attaining it. They are a special brotherhood as Team 134. In the family, creating a family identity forms centricity—brotherhood and sisterhood.

Paul says when you find someone in sin, "restore him gently. But watch yourself, or you also may be tempted" (Gal. 6:1). He understands peer pressure, the power of others' behavior becoming our own. That is also the strength of the family. It's why family identity is invaluable.

If the whole world falls away, my family knows Demsicks remain strong, and they are encouraged. If the church chooses compromise over God's Word, they take solace that Demsicks are sold out and will follow God whole-heartedly. We receive support from who we are together, much as we receive support from being connected to all Christians. We are part of the body of Christ. But we buy into the family vision, too.

Many Christians mistakenly think Jesus placed no emphasis on family. When Jesus asked, "Who is my mother, and who are my brothers?" (Matt. 12:48) he shifted the focus from a son in his earthly family to one as God's Son. He was making a point about what matters eternally, not undermining the natural family. But when a family follows Christ, the family identity is essential. It is a vehicle for spiritual growth that points everyone to Christ. God doesn't devalue it. It is a reflection of the relationship between the Father and the Son.

Instead, Jesus tells Christians who give to the church over their parents they are wicked. They should "honor [their] father and mother" (Matt. 15:4) and provide for their needs even before tithing. Proverbs tells of a "friend who sticks closer than a brother" (Prov. 18:24), because brotherhood is such an intimate relationship. Jesus' care for his own mother culminates at the cross when he tells John, "Here is your mother" (John 19:27). He shows the relationship of a son needs to be replaced. God wishes us to derive identity from these relationships when they glorify him, much as we identify with the family of God, and in his family, give him glory.

Forming an identity is invaluable in discipling a family.

In it, a man sets a specific vision based on extensive study of the Word of God. He leads the family to maturity and real relationship with God. Then he creates a family identity of what it means to be [their name] that reinforces the bond of who they are in Christ and sets the standard.

A specific identity with a specific vision.

Michigan and Team 134.

THE TRADITIONS OF GODLY MEN

To many Christians, "tradition" is a dirty word. It rings hollow as dead or archaic. Something irrelevant. Possibly even dangerous. However, the opposite is true if it is an effective tradition. Traditions remind us of the way. They show meaning.

The problem is when traditions lose their meaning and people go on maintaining them. It's no good to read the same prayer over and over without thinking about it. It's useless to celebrate holidays or festivals and not reflect on what they represent. Even communion is worthless without remembering the Savior. Actually, it *is* dangerous—people have died for not respecting it in the manner it commands.

Let's set the record straight. The Pharisees were not accused of following traditions, but of supplanting the Word of God *for* the traditions of men. Throughout his Word, God commanded his people to observe certain traditions *so they would never forget* what he has done.

For the same reason, traditions are crucial in a family identity. Whatever is true about being a Demsick is also true about being a Christian. But we've put traditions in place as specific road markers that remind our family of who we are in Christ along the way.

Effective traditions create patterns that focus on God. One tradition we celebrate is Passover. The Jews have held Passover every year since their departure from Egypt. In astounding rising action up to the cross, right on time, Jesus celebrated this meal with his disciples the night before he was crucified. It was the moment the tradition had pointed to for thousands of years. The Passover Lamb would be sacrificed.

A tradition that has lost its meaning is St. Patty's Day. Centuries ago, a man named Patrick brought revival to God sweeping across Ireland. Now, all people do is get drunk on that day, and I doubt many know what they're celebrating. I wonder how many tell Patrick's story and encourage each other to be bold witnesses for Christ. In contrast, my brothers and I raise a glass on that day. We toast, "To Jesus," as we knowingly look into each others' eyes. We remind each other who we boldly live for. I think of Jesus raising a glass and honoring God with it, daring to be different from the culture. *Whether you eat or drink or whatever you do, do it all for the glory of God* (1 Cor. 10:31). We do not vilify what Jesus made holy; we simply make it holy. All traditions of worth point to him.

But if a person gets drunk on St. Patty's Day and stumbles into the world's crowd, he changes no one. He impresses no one.

Traditions are important landmarks. Rich meaning should be infused into them. Yet they're worth nothing without regular, deep teaching. In the family, if tailored to meet the vision of leading the family in Christ, they are powerful. Our parents reminded us of the meanings of traditions they chose for us. We loved them. In time, they began to define who we were. And that's a good thing.

One tradition Angela's family had was to take the boat and jet skis out on the river every Monday. Being a pastor's kid, her weekends were focused on ministry and paced right around the speed of light. But Monday—Monday was all family.

There's something therapeutic about basking in the sun while spray shoots up from the hull of one's jet ski, leaving a churning wake in its path. Stress melts and whisks away with the gentle coastal breeze. Majestic pines, sparsely clustered with needles, beckon from far off islands to share secrets kept for the passer-by who slows long enough to listen to the wind whistling through their branches. A tradition upon these waters reminds two girls they come before work and hustle and the busyness of life.

Once a year, Mom and Dad snuck me and my three brothers away from school to the Toledo Zoo. Bears clambering up mountainous terrain, a tiger brooding beneath the shade of a rock ledge, all became larger than life. One wondered what the great cat might do if found in the wild or if the door to his cage suddenly swung open.

But the most powerful experience was not found in a cage or explained on a plaque on display. It was in a car ride or walk up to the front gate by boys who learned family was more important than school. Important enough to abandon the world for a day. We looked forward to the trip every year, an annual reminder our family came first. And we heard the message loud and clear.

A family with a tradition of taking the boat on the river or a day off school to visit the zoo is one that builds lifelong bonds. These bonds will hold when brothers skin their knees in backyard brawls, when girls hug Mom and Dad good-bye and pack for college.

Traditions, if they break out of the mold, become highlights of the year everyone anticipates. A tradition of reading the Bible Christmas morning *before* opening presents—the prophecy in Isaiah 9, Zechariah losing his speech, the angel's visit to Mary, the birth of Jesus, and the blessing of Simeon—leaves an impression of priorities that lasts for a lifetime. And it may just become a turning point in a little one's life.

Through each landmark my parents chose, I fell more in love with God as the road markers pointed me closer to him.

But they would've meant nothing if my parents hadn't deeply loved God. If they'd grumbled through Advent calendar readings because dinner was getting cold or lit candles without discussing their significance, if they'd complained or fought during prayer times, the traditions wouldn't have brought my heart any nearer to Christ in all his glory.

But my parents did use them to lead us to Christ. Each one fit the family vision perfectly. That's the beauty of this principle. Every family is different. You can make the traditions your own.

If you connect your traditions with your family blueprint, you'll find, as your family falls in love with them, they'll fall more in love with Christ. If you point your family to him, their passion and anticipation for him will only grow. And you will find worthwhile the traditions of godly men.

STEWARD OF THE MYSTERY

Yet, training isn't always fun and games. Inevitably, fights and difficulties come. At these times, a man must take charge, steering his family in the right direction. Back to the vision.

When a man notices problems, he reminds his family who they are and the right way to act. He has an order he is always ready to train. If he wants to disciple a character quality or truth, he brings them to the Word. He explains, teaches, and models it for them.

A man and his wife do this with the children. Any behavior or thought that negatively impacts their maturity in Christ must be addressed. At times, a man does this with his wife, as well. He notices negative attitudes or behaviors in her, so he brings her to the Word.

A classic mistake of family headship is to believe the ideal scenario is to be without conflict. That is *not* the goal. Conflict is a good thing; it reveals our deeper issues and beliefs. When a man sees his wife or children need to grow, he *must* say something; he has to deal with it and the truths behind it, not sweep it into the growing mound under the rug.

Dismissing negative behaviors is like a coach who overlooks poor technique because he doesn't want to cause problems with his players. They'll never have excellent form if he doesn't re-teach when they miss it.

When a man lets issues slide and dismisses signs of deeper problems, they'll come back, as Obi-Wan says in *Star Wars: A New Hope* of the Sand People, "and in greater number."

Behavior comes from character. It reveals it. Sometimes a man faces fierce battles to set a higher standard of what he knows is right for his family. Every man reaches the point when he realizes taking on a certain battle could become—pardon me—hell on earth, and he's tempted to compromise the vision God has given him for his family. The irony is it will be worse if he *doesn't* stick to it, because of what it produces in the family. And his family will eventually follow if he perseveres.

Remember, the goal is not to maintain peace but to "[teach] everyone with all wisdom, so that [he] may present everyone perfect in Christ" (Col. 1:28).

Ignoring conflicts that cool or the character issues that cause them buries the mina God gave him in the ground. It is spiritually irresponsible.

A man pastors to the extent he loves.

I have seen my wife grow immeasurably from this vision and leadership; it has been such a blessing to her and to our relationship. So many times early on we'd fight and I'd want to talk about it. She'd roll her eyes at me, or I'd speak abruptly. Then, we'd discuss, go over the right way to act, ask forgiveness and forgive, and grow to become complete—mature in Christ.

And it's my responsibility to train and lead in this. Even by asking forgiveness.

My wife used to dread the talks because she knew we were in for a long, drawn-out conversation. I love them. I keep my eye on the prize. The investment it takes to work through problems, repent and forgive, and train godly behavior produces a rich harvest in due time. We've both grown from it. More profoundly, our intimacy has grown, as well.

Now if you ask Angela about all the talks, the times I haven't let an argument go or we've explored the early hours of the morning, the times we've opened the Word or practiced mature responses, she'd say she wouldn't have it any other way. Not anymore. She'd also say she never knew how much women whose husbands don't take on their full role are missing.

You see, after we were married, Angela let me in on a secret. She explained the quality she was most looking for in a godly husband was one who was strong. She looked around at the men of our culture—I have to add, sadly—the men of our church, and decided she wanted a man who would lead her. That should tell us something about godly women.

Women of God aren't trying to escape male leadership; they're searching for it. They're looking for strong, godly men. They might struggle in the moment and not want to discuss another comment or attitude. They might balk at the secret weapon of "the talk." But don't be deceived.

When they share about their husbands, godly women don't complain about men who bring their wives to the Word, who study it with them and teach them from it. Not if they love them as they do it. No, they talk about it and laugh with a *glow* in their eyes. It is a comfort to their souls. They complain about men who won't open the Word for their families. They complain about men who *won't lead them*.

-Chapter Eleven-

THE OAK AND ITS SPRINKLER SYSTEM

ↄ

Relationships with God…

The trees rustled above me. The canopy of leaves stirred with a slow trickle, each shape tinkling against the next, excited to pass along its gentle whisper.

A steady swell picked up the wind until it rushed through the long, swaying timber that bent as though shaking hands to reintroduce themselves after a forgetful hour apart.

A symphony of sound and motion swept through the treetops.

My mom often disappeared on prayer walks in these dense woods pocketing Interlochen in northern Michigan. I understood why.

It was like God had left this spot on earth as an Eden—a hallowed ground—and those fortunate enough to stumble upon it could commune with him as he'd once intended: in long, ambling walks through oaks and ferns, past forgotten trails and ravines of fallen deadwood, where the soft ground of a marsh yawns as though it almost remembers once being a river, longer ago than most locals would know.

It's a good place to hear his voice quietly speaking, amidst the whisper of the trees.

It is a place, when I have been away, I often long for.

SWEPT UP INTO GOD

I grew up thinking I didn't have a testimony.

My parents raised me knowing Jesus. I can't remember a

time I didn't know him. That makes for a boring story when people get up to share amazing changes of what God has done in their lives. Having no life-altering conversion, no hard drugs, illicit sex, or Ponzi-related scandal, somewhere along the line I became convinced my story wasn't as valid. I knew God, but I didn't have a testimony.

Baptized as an infant. Fell in love with Jesus before the memory of decisions remained. I imagine I was as open as any young kid. My relationship with the One who lives began when I could understand relationships. I don't remember my first choice to accept God. But I make the choice every day to follow. How can I not? I love him.

Jesus said, "When I am lifted up...(I) will draw all men to myself" (John 12:32). He was referring to the cross and salvation.

That's our life goal—to be drawn to him and to draw others, as well.

It's the goal of the family.

The most important thing a man can do is lift up Jesus and encourage people to know him as he truly is. It begins with falling in love with Christ. The end is maturity in him.

Real maturity is being planted firmly in God without the prop of someone else's faith. It is becoming an oak of righteousness to which others can turn for shade under its branches.

An oak's maturity is measured by a root system underneath the ground that spans as large as the tree itself. No drought can kill it. No storm can uproot it. To the extent we grow our relationship with Jesus, we reach these roots deep into the soil of our hearts in every direction.

Also, developing a relationship with God is like learning to fish for a lifetime instead of bumming a bite from the local boys down by the dock every time hunger strikes. It's having one's heart swept up in the river. Being drawn there because the cool breeze, rustle of leaves, trickle of water across the rocks, and shimmer of sunlight off the bottom of the creek bed capture one's heart. The fisherman will fish for a lifetime just to sit beside these waters.

God wants us to be swept up in him like the river.

Like the whispering of a canopy of leaves that, no matter where I am, I can still somehow hear calling.

He wants our roots as deeply planted in him as the thickest oak that quenches its thirst beside the riverbank.

How can one not fall in love with God when a relationship with him is so beautiful—so satisfying?

However, as long as the tree's root system is small and doesn't tap into a constant supply of water, it is susceptible. Likewise, the man won't have reliable provision until he learns to catch his own fish. But when he falls in love with the river, he will never leave its waters.

The mature Christian is like these. He's saturated like the tree that won't send its roots any other direction than the river. He's in love like the man who sits by its banks for a lifetime.

This tree will grow thick and full. This man will eat forever.

This is what a pastor inspires.

For the man who hungers and thirsts after righteousness, it may be the most exciting part of the job. He cultivates a culture of companionship with God and desire for him. Like my mom said, "The greatest purpose in life is to love God and to let him love us."

Creating an environment that inspires this simple love relationship is the job of the pastor of the home.

THE HEART OF A CHILD

From early childhood, I was raised to have this kind of relationship with God. He was near me and loved me and I was made to worship him.

One day after school, in first grade, my parents received a call from my Christian teacher. "John-Peter won't pray," she confided. "When we tell the kids it's time to pray, everyone folds their hands and bows their heads. John-Peter doesn't. He opens his hands and looks up."

"But," my dad replied, "that's how we pray at our house!"

"Oh," the teacher responded and fell silent.

We had many positions for prayer. Each expressed an attitude of worship toward him. I didn't know I was doing anything unusual in class because I was praying as I'd learned at home. My story was formed in the early pages of this worship book and was my own, shaped by a culture of love and worship.

Growing up, we experienced God. We sang songs. We praised God. We declared the names of God. We stood and raised hands. Sometimes we danced. We banged on little instruments. We read the Bible. We listened in silence. And we always loved him.

Years later, I formed a high school prayer group. We channeled our youthful passions into having fun worshiping God. Some of our games included yelling names for God while doing laps around the church parking lot. We pulled in and did God cheers on three like a sports team.

We weren't crazy. We were just crazy for God. And when kids make a relationship with God as unique and passionate as their hearts, it becomes vivid and real.

We have a real God. He wants us to really be in love with him. Like praise laps around parking lots and God cheers.

Like a first-grader opening up little hands and lifting them to the sky to pray.

This births the single most important advice I have ever given parents: take daily worship times as a family in which you experience God's love and whole-heartedly praise him together. I was given that and grew up knowing Christ. I cannot think of a better way to raise children to know and love God.

And that is my testimony.

WORSHIP TIMES

You can lead a horse to water, but you can't make him drink. Apparently. The janitor of my church in Michigan years ago said the common cliché is wrong. If you want to make a horse drink, all you have to do is give it a lick of salt. A wise old guy. After that salt, nothing can keep the horse from lapping up the water.

In a way, the same is true of God.

Parents can do more than say bedtime prayers and read an occasional Bible story to their children.

They can give them a lick of salt.

The Psalmist says, "Taste and see that the Lord is good; blessed is the man who takes refuge in him" (Psalm 34:8).

Jesus said, "I tell you the truth, you are looking for me, not because you saw miraculous signs but because you ate the loaves and had your fill" (John 6:26). Besides the bread he gave them, he was referring to how they hungered for God and were filled, which was more important than all the signs and wonders they saw him perform.

Revelation adds, "The Spirit and the bride say, 'Come!' And let him who hears say, 'Come!' Whoever is thirsty, let him come; and whoever wishes, let him take the free gift of the water of life" (Rev. 22:17).

There's a connection between worshiping God, knowing him, and loving him forever. Once one has experienced a taste of his love, one is unlikely to go back to ordinary, worldly sustenance.

Is this what you are offering your family? Are you inviting your wife and children into a rich, deep, satisfying relationship with Christ that fulfills the longings of their souls?

When a man introduces his family to Christ, they will want to drink deeply of God. They will hunger for him. They will thirst for his Word and Spirit. With an appetite that grows for a lifetime.

One finds it in family worship. A few licks of salt.

MY STORY

Worship times in the Demsick house were a blast. We called them "prayer times." Twenty minutes a day, we transformed into a family band (usually out of key and offbeat). You can probably imagine the exuberance (and loudness) of a family of four boys expressing love for God the only way they know how. We were all smiles and laughter, banging away on cheap instruments as Mom led with her guitar. Dad rapped on the conga to his one beat. We danced around to family favorites, sometimes wildly—riotously, even—but always passionately worshiping God. We shouted and spoke praises in adoration. God was near; he loved us and we loved him.

So, for our family, church was six Demsicks bounding around the living room. We went to church on Sunday, too, and loved it. But I think we were more passionate there because we worshiped together as a family every day of the week.

We tasted God.

Years later, there was no stuffy old church for me to leave when I turned eighteen. No constraints of my parents' beliefs to shed when I moved out of the house. I grew up worshiping God. I loved him. I *knew* him.

We had fun with God every day. That's what daily worship is all about. But, still, there was nothing haphazard about it; we were trained in it.

FAMILY WORSHIP

I've learned the one most crucial skill in worship is probably also the most uncomfortable. Every Christian must learn to pray *out loud*. People cringe at the thought of speaking in front of others, especially in open worship. But it's vital to encouraging others' faith and creating an atmosphere of worship. When one prays silently, God hears, and it encourages the person praying. But when one prays out loud, every person is built up through hearing, and they can pray along, as well.

Become an active worshiper. Worship stales quickly if everyone sits around waiting for someone else to say something. Vocal prayer creates an atmosphere of worship, whether one prays at a time or all praise together. It turns everyone's hearts to him.

Let me be honest in this. I don't think it's optional for the strong Christian. Please understand, private faith is somewhat of an illusion; we are meant to interact with others. That's why the psalmist says, "Shout aloud to the Rock of our Salvation," (Psalm 95:1) and, "Shout for joy to the Lord" (100:1, 98:4). It's also why David danced publicly before God. There are times when we need to praise him together.

When you do, you'll find prayer times become powerful. You ignite your passion and others catch it. You agree in prayer and inspire each other. Praise with six people who pray boldly becomes infectious as everyone worships God passionately. Without words, the same six enter the doldrums. Think how many times you've fallen asleep while praying silently on your pillow.

As an experiment, I once told a teenager to pray silently while the others in his group prayed along in their heads. After fifteen seconds of awkward silence, I stopped the bewildered student who was supposedly praying. Curious, I asked everyone how praying along went. The responses were…interesting. The ticking clock. Spacing out. We tried it again out loud and it went much better.

The truth is praying aloud is a skill to practice. And it can be exciting. You'd be surprised how much kids enjoy being adventurous for God by yelling "Jesus!" at the top of their lungs. A family shout-to-the-Lord session is freeing. Make it a game and see who can pray out the most names for God in ten seconds. Your kids may forget their shyness (if they have any) and join in to try to win. You may, too. Do a family shout on a countdown (3-2-1-shout) with a favorite praise, a laughable way to get kids comfortable praising God out loud. Egg them on to make the neighbors hear it and you may just have some radical, budding lovers of Christ on your hands.

You can find ways that work best for your family. However, no game will replace you modeling worship for them. As the family pastor, you must lead in this. And once the family gains confidence, you will have powerful prayer times.

Additionally, I recommend 75-85% of a prayer time be spent singing worship songs and speaking praises aloud to God. The basis for our relationship with God is love and we should spend our time loving him together. The other 15-25% should be praying for people's needs and a minute or two spent listening to God. Too much time listening, especially when it exceeds time reading the Bible, can distract from a simple love relationship built on the Word. God doesn't have difficulty reaching us. If he doesn't say anything, he wants you to have faith in him and know he loves you.

The final tip about family worship is the real secret. Prayer times should be fun. Yep, that's it.

Demsick prayer times featured songs that were part of our family identity. "Ghost Riders," by Johnny Cash showed up often. We rode imaginary horses around the living room and cracked whips as we sang a song about a cowboy getting right with God. I suppose that's how a family of four boys learns to worship God. Another song, "The Dancing Heart" inspired leaping, running, and dancing before the Lord that ended with four huffing little boys with tired bodies and happy hearts. During "Behold, How Good and Pleasant It Is," an Israeli folk song, we paced in a circle, swayed back and forth, and clasped hands in the center. The clasps increased until they became punches. Those were prayer times. The laughter and joy that followed defined us as men and as brothers. God appealed to our hearts.

I remember at one point the family got out of the habit of doing prayer times. Someone requested we bring them back, and pretty soon we were worshiping daily again. They were dancing, singing, instrument pounding, praise declaring, shouting, listening, God-filled, intimate, heart-changing worship times. I vividly remember God's presence filling our little living room as we stood and praised with arms raised. I remember it as we quietly sat and worshiped in our hearts. Prayer times drew us together. They drew us to God.

All you need to start them is a guitar, a three or four song worship set on a computer or ipod, or a continuous worship radio station. Add a few toy instruments for the kids and you have the essentials for family worship. You may not make a beautiful sound, but you'll raise a family of worshipers. There were plenty of times growing up when all I added was banging a stick on a wood block. But those were precious times to God. So let the joyful clunking begin. An atmosphere of exploration and freedom without shame is the perfect environment to train bold lovers of Christ.

What songs get your family riled up? Are there deep, worshipful ones you love and fun ones that make you laugh? As the pastor and worship leader, it's your job to tailor prayer times to fit the vision and family personality to bring everyone closer to Christ.

20 minutes a day. A constant watering of the Holy Spirit and worship that continues steady growth in God for a lifetime.

If a man builds a sprinkler system into his lawn, he'll never have to lug out the hose again. The job will continue to be done. If a man builds worship habits for close relationship with

God in his family's lives, he won't have to worry about maintaining it later in life. As their love for God and discipline grow, they will water their own lives permanently.

To review the simple tips for worship times:

1) Learn to praise out loud
2) Worship and praise God 75% or more of the time
3) Make it fun

These aren't rules or legalism, but powerful principles that, if applied, will reap a 10, 20, 30 or 100 fold harvest in the hearts of the family members in which they are planted. And they'll bring the family together in a bond of love nothing else could. With the Lover of the universe.

THE HORSE AND ITS WATER

I was thinking the other day how fresh God is to a child, but how many doubts creep in as we reach adulthood. Thoughts tempt us we never imagined would. And if we don't experience regular time with God, it's easy to doubt he's there or what we believed when we were young is true. If we spend time with him in a fresh, new way, those doubts are quickly cast aside. They have nowhere to grow roots, because we *know* God.

You remember a friend you see often. You remember one you spend a significant amount of time with. More than anything, you remember a best friend.

That's what God should be. We won't lose our grasp on him or our beliefs in his Word if we spend time with him and make him our best friend. Actually, everything about God will become second nature to us. But the friends we knew in childhood, the ones in faded photographs who we haven't seen in years, start to slip away. We don't really know anymore. We forget.

The Bible says, "Train up a child in the way he should go, and when he's old he will not depart..." (Prov. 22:6, KJV).

When children are trained to apply the fertilizer of worship and water of the Word daily and experience the joy of a luxuriant, lush garden, years later they will never want to go back to weeds and dry ground.

Like the horse, they can be led to water, and they will drink. They just need a lick of salt.

MAKE THE BIBLE COME ALIVE

I was nine years old. My younger brothers and I crowded around the living room entertainment center, curled up on the fuzzy, matted carpet. A husky voice growled from the dual cassette stereo speakers. "And the conspirators rejoiced...." Sounds of murmuring and mischievous revelry whet our anticipation.

"Daniel!" The voiced rumbled. "Did your God save you?"

Burl Ives thundered right out of those speakers and into our hearts.

We were mesmerized. Daniel and the lion's den. David and Goliath. Jonah. Stories larger than a child's world came to life and lit up our imaginations. We fought against the conspirators with Daniel. We faced the giant with David. We gulped for breath on the beach with Jonah. And each story sank into our hearts, making an indelible impression there.

Years later, I went back and searched for those tales. The complete sets could not be found. Burl Ives and his legendary Bible story tapes had slipped into the silent past, quietly forgotten amongst decades of unraveled cassettes and discontinued books. But the stories he told there have not been forgotten.

When my three brothers and I get together, we still quote those lines between laughs. The stories still echo in our hearts.

That's the power of bringing the Bible to life. They are God's stories, the most perfectly crafted plotlines, from the deception of a snake in the garden to the storming of the world by a man on a white horse, charging toward a war he's already won.

Gideon and glass jars. God cuts an army to a handful. Joshua and Jericho. The walls come crashing down. A field of dry bones comes to life. A woman's beauty captures a king and frees a kingdom. A baby is born in straw and hay who angels tell will save the world.

That's the Bible. It's true. And it will change our lives.

In the wide-eyed, wild imaginations of our children, it will form theirs.

Build a life, shape a destiny. Shape a child and change the world.

While our worlds are still small and filled with wonder, the Lord is a hero every child wants to follow. Impress the beauty of the Word upon a child's heart in all its glory during those early years, and that child will honor God long after her jeans have lengthened or he's left home to conquer the world.

Even an adult's world can be transformed by them. Apply a little perspective to the Word and romance and passion leap off the pages. It's filled with intrigue, adventure, heartbreak, and daring rescue. The bad guys couldn't be more devious nor the good guys more heroic. And real.

Kind of makes you want to be like them.

Amidst the routine of life is the mission to make this fantastical world our own. That is transforming one's mind and renewing one's life.

"Do not conform any longer to the pattern of this world, but be transformed by the renewing of your mind" (Rom. 12:2).

Do not languish anymore with the perspective of darkened minds, but be inspired by God's dreams as he unveils passion before your eyes.

Besides restoring truth, God's Word restores the hope that moves the human heart.

It is a grain of sand on a beach that becomes a star in the sky and lights up the destiny of a nation in a man's eyes. It is a shiny glint along the shore of every thought God has towards you.

Read it often. Read it with your children.

Take a grain of sand and place it in a jar alongside a child's bed and it will set the ocean in his heart. Teach the child her destiny and it will light the nightscape in her eyes.

Plant the Word of God in a child's heart, and you will see it grow into a tree that provides leaves for the healing of the nations and his own heart, as well.

The seed can begin as early as there is a spark in a child's eyes. Her first words can be from her first Bible. His first dreams can be of conquering giants. And you will birth a man or woman who becomes an oak of righteousness, whose roots break through walls and in whose branches the birds of the air will come and find rest.

-Chapter Twelve-
LOVE IN CHAMPAGNE BOTTLES

Family Relationships…

The sun had almost set over the ocean from the cliffs of Jamaica. Our round hut, built entirely out of rock with a thatch roof, overlooked a breathtaking 180 degree vista of ocean that seemed to extend forever. The fading light split the sky, cut through cumulus clouds that hovered lazily in the distance, and splintered into brilliant shades of orange and red slivers that shone across the horizon.

An old wood bridge hung thirty feet above clear, teal waters and extended over a cavern cut into the rocks. It was the entrance to this cliff-side paradise.

And the escape? The bridge. Or a quick plunge into cool, refreshing waters below. From the front door.

Angela stunned in her elegant evening gown, and I chose slacks and a nice button down shirt and tie. Although no one would know besides us (and a resident bat or two), we wanted the night to be special.

Dinner arrived—lobster with a side of Jamaican-style vegetables and champagne. The sun blinked its last ray and quietly slipped beneath the surface of the world, leaving us with just the flicker of a candle and the light in our eyes.

A romantic night like this can't be topped, so we chose to repeat it, ordering lobster and champagne to cliff-side hut again the next. It was the most beautiful honeymoon we could've imagined.

Can anything compare to it?

Well, possibly real life.

Though we can't afford the accommodations, God desires we maintain, even *increase*, this romance.

THE GREATEST OF THESE IS LOVE

No matter what life is like, there's one thing I can do to guarantee Angela's day gets a little better. I can love her.

A little note conspicuously left where she will find it. A carefully selected bouquet of flowers that send a message her heart longs to hear. A bath set up with candles and music. Anything with a little thought.

Cleaning the dishes in the sink *and* running the garbage disposal.

Okay, that one might not be as romantic. But you'd be surprised what a difference it makes.

Angela wants to know I care, and every effort I make to show her matters. As men, our teaching and traditions, our vision and leadership, all are worth nothing without our love.

"If I know all mysteries and all knowledge…but do not have love, I am nothing" (1 Cor. 13:2, NASB).

My wife shares with me that, at her lowest, it's nice to know God loves and values her, but what she really wants to hear is that I love her. My love comforts her. It is something I hope to give her innumerable ways over the course of her lifetime.

Nothing I do to lead or disciple would have any effect if she didn't know I love her. Actually, the reason I lead and disciple is because I love. I care enough to want my family to grow, to see each mature into a complete man or woman in Christ. It's the heart of a shepherd.

But it's not enough to want them to grow without wanting *them*. Every good husband and father does. The hard part is proving it in the daily schedule. My dad wisely says family relationships is the one area quality time isn't a replacement for quantity time.

We have to prioritize our wives and children. If our relationships with them shift to auto-pilot, they will sense the growing neglect and perceive it as a lack of love.

I spent a week distant from my wife because I was sick and she was pregnant. Separate couches and no kissing. I wouldn't hold her hand. I had a feeling the week wouldn't end well, but I didn't want a sick, pregnant wife. I was right about the result. Instead I had an indignant, pregnant wife.

It was a problem intimacy, affection, and the prettiest flowers would solve.

But there's a lesson in it. She needs me; she needs my constant love.

How different is the kid whose eyes beg for Dad to scoop him up as he plops in front of the TV after a long day at work?

It is a continuous need.

And though hard, it's a simple choice, because we love them.

I spoke of honeymoon love, but it's not the complete picture. There is a love that is far more valuable. It's a love that carried its cross to a hill and died there.

In *The Cost of Discipleship,* Dietrich Bonhoffer writes, "When Christ calls a man, he bids him come and die." Christ's call is to follow in his footsteps to the cross. Jesus says, "He must deny himself and take up his cross and follow me" (Matt. 16:24).

But, lest we misunderstand, that's *life.* Out-of-your-chest, joy-filled, heart-thumping passion. It was "for the joy set before him Christ endured the cross, scorning its shame" (Heb. 12:2). God wants our hearts to experience this same joy; only the selfishness needs to die.

That's how a husband loves a wife and a father loves a child.

Ephesians 5:25 says, "Husbands, love your wives, just as Christ also loved the church and gave Himself up for her."

Christ's love isn't an emotion on a Mother's Day card. It lays its life down on a cross and picks it up again "to draw all men to [himself]" (John 12:32).

Husbands are called to do the same.

The kind of love that saves the world is the only kind worthy of our families. This kind makes the full journey to Golgotha, coming "not to be served, but to serve" (Matt. 20:28). And though it sacrifices itself on a cross, it spends no more time in tombs than Lazarus. Than Jesus. For with it comes victory.

A love like this can save a family.

When I was a college student, I began the habit of washing my parents' dishes and wiping down their countertops after visiting them. They usually had just fed me. But I was often tired and preferred to stretch my legs on the couch and let someone else see to it later. I did it to practice.

It may sound strange, but, to me, serving my parents was practice for my future wife. I knew if I helped them, I'd be better prepared to serve her when it was difficult. I was deliberately forming character.

Jesus didn't want to carry the cross. He was tired. He was in a lot of pain. But he did it anyway because he loved her. His Bride. Us.

That's love. It's not merely a feeling or desire. It isn't presented on a platter with lobster or champagne by candlelight. That may be one part. There is enchanting romance to love. But, more pressingly, it's a choice to put another before oneself.

A young college student who should've been roof jumping or annoying the late night staff at Denny's washed his parents' dishes and strengthened a discipline that might come in useful later in life.

Now that I'm married, Angela may serve me more than I do her. However, it's God's desire I lead in this. It's something all men should practice.

Our wives won't mind too much.

When Christ calls a man, he bids him come and die.

When Christ calls a husband, he bids him come and give himself up for his bride.

It's not that different. The call to be a husband and father, while a call to death, is a call to life. Real *satisfaction*. To joy that perseveres through everything—the kind of love only a selfless man is capable of. It's a kind women and children are desperate for.

It plays with his kids. It puts his wife first. It spends *quantity* time with them. It adores her.

It's a force to be reckoned with in the family. It's a power unparalleled in a marriage.

When Christ calls a man, he bids him come and die.

When a man calls a wife, like Christ does for the church, he bids her come and be died for.

He bids her come and be loved.

COMMUNITIES OF LOVE

Jesus identified the two greatest commandments as, "Love the Lord your God..." and "Love your neighbor as yourself" (Matt. 22:37,39).

That comes from the top. It started with him.

Just as from the top down God loved the world and Christ loved us, the responsibility to love in the family starts at the top. Men love first. Their love fuels the family. In response, everyone else loves. It's no surprise men are called to greater sacrifice in laying down their lives for their wives. For, "greater love has no one than this, that he lay down his life for his friends" (John 15:13).

They say the behavior of a church is usually a product of the behavior of the pastor. The church's character mirrors his. His shortcomings hinder them from growing. His strengths increase their own. This fits when one understands discipleship—the culture a leader sets and how his role has real purpose. The same applies to the family. If true, we need to take a long look at our reflection mirrored there. Are we exhibiting selfless, mature love in everything? Are we building a community of love that starts with us?

Love begins with the leader. It occurs to me, the life of a church or family is really a simple, childhood game of follow the leader.

We need to actively create communities of love.

In those communities, friends become brothers for a lifetime.

Brothers become best friends forever.

And the church and family become lovers of Christ whose bonds will never be broken.

TIME TOGETHERS

Yet, building relationships isn't complicated. One of the things we loved as boys was what Dad called "time-togethers." On a given day of the week, Dad would rotate going out with one of the four of us. He took us out individually to make us feel special and develop close relationships with us. The classic time-together was chopping wood at the lumber yard and cooling off with root beer floats at A&W. We'd crank up the chainsaw and work 'til we smelled like wood chips. After an exhausting, sweaty day, we'd suck down cold root beer and spoon smooth ice cream sludge into our mouths just as he had with his father.

We loved those times with Dad.

Dad reminded me recently of a campground he took us to when we were young. We'd soak in the Jacuzzi or navigate mini-golf balls around a sand trap and pond. Or plop them right in.

"You took just one of us at a time?"

"Oh, absolutely," he nodded, as though it were taken for granted.

Time-togethers made us feel important. They let us know Dad loved us.

They're vital to do with sons and daughters. A date with a daughter is a moment she will never forget. She transforms into a princess at the ball, Cinderella to her prince. An adventure with a son impresses on his heart the daring nature he shares with his dad. It tells him, "*You're a son after my own heart. A hero like me.*" Kids need to know they matter enough for the world to stop spinning, now and then, for them to become the center of a more imaginative universe.

Wives do too. No matter how busy life gets, a couple must make date night romantic. They may not recreate Paris or the cliffs of Jamaica, but light a candle and strike up the orchestra and they can come close. More than doing any chore, shuttling to trombone lessons, or trimming the front landscape, a man needs to love his wife. Even more than their kids, she's his first priority.

So many couples get this backwards. They focus on the kids so much they find themselves looking back years later and wondering where the passion went. It may have gone to soccer practice. Quite realistically, it may have slipped out the back between work and routine when no one was paying attention. It's a temptation one must resist to live for the kids and neglect one's spouse. One of the great lessons my parents showed us as kids was we were second. We knew Mom was most important to Dad, and he was to her. And we *loved it.*

Kids pout and scream and throw temper tantrums when the world doesn't revolve around them, but deep down that isn't what they want. It would make them miserable. What they really want is to feel secure. When Mom honored Dad and Dad adored her, it made us feel good. We were in a safe place. The world didn't revolve around us, and we didn't need it to. We just wanted to be a part of their world. And because they put their marriage first, it was a beautiful place to live with them.

Don't ever lose date night or the spontaneous little things that bring you together, and let the romance with your wife fizzle.

A note on her pillow reminds her the fairy tale lives on. It tells her she's still the princess of your heart, though she has become queen. Tuck secrets away for her to find that she'll relish later. Display your love for her boldly. Don't serve the kids to her neglect.

Your relationship with her is core to the family.

CENTERING THE FAMILY

But bonding the Beauty and the kids of the kingdom is important, too. To develop a family into a community of love, like the individuals, they need "time-togethers," both spiritual and fun.

Read the Bible, huddled up on the couch. Do devotions on the kids' bedroom floor. Discuss God around the dinner table—you know, the monolith in the dining room that goes unused except for Thanksgiving and Christmas. Go to church together.

My favorite memory from church is having my arms raised, praising God, singing at the top of my lungs, and looking down the row at my brothers who were praising just as passionately as me. It's the most inspiring moment I've experienced in church, yet it happened regularly.

Angela tells how she and her sister joined their parents at Christian conferences when they were young. I can imagine the excitement with which they tossed ideas back and forth from the day's events as they plopped down on their beds for the evening. What a way to bond as a family over spiritual matters.

The Demsick clan went to Christian wrestling camps. My favorite part was the nights, when we'd sneak out of our rooms and stay up with the few renegade men who wanted to sing worship songs and talk about God into the late hours. Those were passionate nights that fed my desire to be a man of God.

During one of the testimonies at those camps, my youngest brother, Richard, decided to set Jesus on the throne of his heart and surrender his life to him forever.

Around the same time, at another camp, my wife-to-be was making her own decision to live sold-out for God.

I wonder how our lives might be different today had our families not prioritized bonding together in exciting adventures for God.

Friendship and love grow deep in families that share this sense of purpose together. They become centered on faith that is real and missional.

FAMILY NIGHTS

Yet, time-togethers should be fun.

On Saturday evenings growing up, we laid out family games. Little pieces chased each other across board games, cars shot up and twisted around tracks, or knights patrolled Lego castles we built. *Charades*, *Fictionary*, and even the old slide projector set the stage for antics and wit that had us bursting in laughter or cringing at naked pictures of me and my female cousin in the kiddy pool.

One that has survived to this day is a game called Skittles. In it, a person pulls a cord that shoots out a top and knocks over tiny pins worth various points. It's hard to believe how much fun six adults can have with a spinning top and a bit of luck, but it's riotous.

The other is obstacle croquet. We rig contraptions and traps around the hoops to ratchet up the entertainment level of the old croquet match. Inevitably, there is usually some mallet thrown onto the roof or ball shot against Dad's screen porch to make it memorable.

But the point is, as silly as they may be, we can't get enough of these times. It's our relationships we wind together with cords around a Skittles top. It's our hearts that soar with reckless mallets for the screen porch. We connect when Mom's mallet gently taps her ball down the hill toward the pond. And we always win.

Moments like these flash back to movies and pizza on Friday nights. Munching Benito's slices while watching *Groundhog Day,* because Mom and Dad had the foresight to know our high school friends would hang out at our house if fed free pizza and a steady stream of movie rentals.

They replay camping at the Kentucky Red River Gorge. Stopping at the Holiday Inn with an indoor pool on the drive to Florida during winter. Trekking across dunes to Lake Michigan under the setting sun, inching its way to the horizon.

Every summer as children we spent exploring rivers and beaches, piers and boardwalks, and deep, majestic woods on this frontier. Mysteries were hidden, explored, and tucked away again for another summer, another year's adventures to rediscover.

My wife, Angela, believes most people undervalue vacations and the bonds they create. But families must get away from the busyness of life to just enjoy each other.

As I write this, my best friend Luke is coming in from a day at the pool in sunny Florida. Every year, he flies to Disney with his wife and three girls for a week of relaxation. It's a tradition that dates back to his father before him and the memories he has as a boy backlit by exploding fireworks and a purple magic kingdom.

This awe is now his children's. The memories will be theirs, as well.

And once a year, the generations and memories merge under a halo of stars and exploding lights across a magical night sky, and all become children once again.

Moments like these remind us how precious life is. They sweep us away in their profundity. Somewhere across the county line of a great adventure, the difference between child and adult blurs and we whisk away as hearts dancing to the same quiet tune of the distant twinkling stars. With the din of work in the town behind us, we become timeless souls, kids lost in wonder again, at peace with the world. We rejoin our place in a timeless universe, as a community of wonder.

Without the creeping of these quiet waters up the soul's shores, there would be no moment of breathless anticipation. Just the dull, dreary grinding of work upon the wheel that never ceases. And our kids will grow old while our eyes are on it, watching it turn.

Families need to break away from their lives and obligations, from the nonsensical turning of time that spins nothing into threads of powdery fineness. Without freedom to explore the beauty and freshness of the world, the family fades into a backdrop of extras in each other's lives.

It misses the richness of the beautiful souls within it and the light in their eyes that reminds them of what they all share—that at heart, and before God, they are all just children.

When families get away, they find the flicker there, the light that tells a story strikingly similar to their own. In it they find a glint, a smile, a full laugh. They find a friend.

And fathers, mothers, daughters, sons, forget their place in the world for a moment. For just that moment, the world hangs still, and they become one.

THE CHURCH
—Breathing Out—

-Chapter Thirteen-
CAPTAIN AT THE HELM

The beauty of this pageantry leads us to the church, created in Christ to draw his family to himself.

To draw his Bride.

He has great plans for her. She is beloved.

He has written an epic tale and invited her to discover it with him. She has come, though often unwillingly. Yet he is filled with desire to pursue her to the final pages.

He'll go to any measure to woo her. He'll take on any challenge to make her his.

But, oh, how she struggles.

Christ, the Lover, longs to gather his Beauty in his arms and sweep her off to a great adventure.

Tiny droplets hit her window pane, and he stands outside, smiles, and motions for her to join him. She returns a half-hearted smile, a distant look in her eyes, and watches him from beyond the glass.

She never fully engages.

The woman by the window could be radiant, but she lacks the willingness to leave her comfort and slosh through the rain that would make her *glisten*.

If she only understood it's life he invites her into...

Sure, it'll be nasty out there. One doesn't run through the rain without getting a little wet. It's uncomfortable, awkward, soggy, and *freeing*.

The only way to experience true life is to run right out, Ralph Laurens, TOMS, and all.

The adventure awaits.

The Love of her life beckons.

If she risks it all, no possibility is too great.

Oh, she can stay inside where it's warm and comfortable. But the inconvenience of water-logged boat shoes and ruined day plans is nothing like the pain of the silent ache that there must be something more beyond the ticking drips upon the pane.

And there is.

Soaking, splashing, drenching...joy. The arms of a Lover whose embrace invites unparalleled passion.

Of a kicking, shouting, dancing, skipping, singing-in-the-rain sort of love.

And of life fully lived.

If she takes it, she'll wonder why she ever considered pausing for coat and umbrella at the door.

That is the choice before us. We are the church. We can choose to remain comfortable or follow. One will preserve the sheen on our shoes and keep mud off the carpet. The other will free us. Our Lover is waiting.

The final three chapters point the way.

THE RIGHT STARTING POINT

This band of starry-eyed dreamers' adventure has a beginning. It has a starting point, a place of embarkation, from which it sets out to change the world.

Everything hinges on that. A few degrees of the compass off equates to hundreds of miles from the destination once the journey is undertaken.

Its success rests in the hands of the captain who holds the compass and charts the course.

It rests in the leaders we choose.

No great organization can achieve beyond the capacity of its leaders.

If a church is the sum of its individuals, then the way

those parts fit together matters. God takes mature men who are successful in the family, who have been faithful with five minas, and he gives them five more. He takes men who have grown their children to maturity in the faith, and he gives them the church.

Take a look at the qualifications for choosing overseers, or pastors:

> An overseer, then, must be above reproach, the husband of one wife, temperate, prudent, respectable, hospitable, able to teach, not addicted to wine or pugnacious, but gentle, peaceable, free from the love of money. He must be one who manages his own household well, keeping his children under control with all dignity (but if a man does not know how to manage his own household, how will he take care of the church of God?), and not a new convert, so that he will not become conceited and fall into the condemnation incurred by the devil. And he must have a good reputation with those outside the church, so that he will not fall into reproach and the snare of the devil. (1 Tim. 3:2-7)

Basically, a pastor must be mature in his life and faith. If he doesn't know what maturity is and how to reach it, the church cannot get there. I know I am being blunt, but we should see the logic in these instructions. There is a connection between the purpose of the church (to bring to maturity in Christ) and the men we choose to lead it.

However, there is another element in the qualifications above. One must also have proven one's success in running a household.

The progression of the family and church is revealed here. Every man is the pastor of his home. Paul tells Timothy to choose men who lead well there to be pastors of the church.

That's God's criteria as the required developmental program for the church. In the business world, we call this a promotion—they've proven their worth. In the church, it's common sense.

Interestingly, this simple path for church growth is often ignored. Do you see how logical it should be? But today, there are men who have mismanaged families yet run the church. And willing congregants populate the pews who don't realize they'll replicate the same result in them.

Now, hang on. Before you start throwing tomatoes (or stones), think about it. Paul isn't being harsh or dictatorial. He's being wise. One should pastor the little church of one's family with success *before* one is promoted to a larger church.

Pastors feel called to ministry. It's important they do. They sense the urgency or hear God speak to them about his plan for their lives. But when the Word of God specifically states the criteria, God's call won't contradict it. He doesn't call contrary to his Word.

Let me give an illustration to connect.

I have friends who've told me God led them to their wives, but not to their first wives. To new ones. Now, if their wives were unfaithful or passed away, God certainly may have done that. If not, the Word of God is clear. "But I tell you that anyone who divorces his wife, except for marital unfaithfulness, causes the divorced woman to become an adulteress, and anyone who marries the divorced woman commits adultery" (Matt. 5:32).

When a man marries, his wife becomes his only choice *for life*. If he divorces for any reason other than unfaithfulness, marrying another woman is adultery, no matter how long the papers have been final.

God doesn't shout "Change your partners" like a square dance caller when everyone gets restless. Not even after years have gone by. Or on a do-over when one becomes a Christian. He doesn't lead that way. If the bond is not destroyed by sex (which formed it), a marriage between two people is sacred. It represents the eternal love of Christ and the church.

The point is there are crucial reasons God leads the way he does *for our own good*. He always does so according to his Word. Whether we understand it or not, we should trust him. We should love him enough to obey.

So clearly, he won't call a man to pastor whose character or children's lives are in shambles. There may be a distant call for which he will later be qualified. But no justification can remove that he is 1) mature in Christ, exhibited in certain qualifications, and 2) a successful pastor of his family.

Yet, we've created other paths. The degree is usually the requirement. However, it's foolish for a church to honor seminary degrees or experience *above* calling men based on God's qualifications. It might be a good idea, though unusual today, to simply call men out of other professions who are qualified by God's standards to lead the church.

Unfortunately, those aren't always the top priority. Some pastors have children who've rebelled against their leadership and don't follow the Lord. Nearly all the adult children of a pastor close to me are non-Christians and live in serious dysfunction. When his children are scarred by years of mixed messages about themselves and God, in and out of counseling, and dealing with serious issues, that should be an indicator his place to disciple is in his family. Restoring them should be the goal before taking on the church. This isn't a harsh message, but a proper one. God has an order.

Of course, a pastor shouldn't legalistically be defined by a grown child's decisions. But the pattern in his family is fruit he has produced over time. More than any piece of paper, it's his resume.

And it's crucial we begin at God's standard.

If we don't have the right starting point, we're in real trouble.

COLLATERAL DAMAGE

Recently, a good friend left the ministry.

Relations with the pastor he'd worked for had deteriorated, and it reached the point he needed time away from church ministry. Really, he confided, the pastor's behavior caused the immaturity problems in the church. The church just continued the patterns he started.

And his family should've provided the clues.

His children walked away from God years ago and his wife opposes him serving in ministry even now. Is it any wonder serving under him became a burden?

A respected leader was so disillusioned he left the ministry.

He now works in business.

Similarly, I've heard too many stories of men who leave their wives yet pastor churches. How exactly is that managing one's own household? Paul indicates "husband of one wife." That isn't a qualification to specifically eliminate polygamists. It also means husbands who haven't left one or two women behind as collateral damage. Now, I know, a man can change and become mature. But, honestly, it takes many years to go from the lack of character of abandoning a spouse or raising spiritually rebellious children to become a man capable of leading the church. Character is built slowly through small, difficult, godly choices. And pastoring isn't about being skilled, but passing on maturity.

Yet this process and the time it takes are often brushed aside.

One pastor I know slept with a woman in his congregation, stepped down, and a year later was leading a Bible study of people from the same church. Wisdom says he should be in another leader's Bible study growing.

Another not far from me had an affair with a woman in his congregation, left his wife, married the mistress, and *still pastors the church to this day*. He never even took a break from ministry. There was a split, but some of the congregation stayed with him. A pastor's job is to bring the Bride to perfection, "without spot or blemish," yet this man abandoned his own bride. Does actual godliness matter? What a state we are in!

God's directions are simple. They make sense. He desires a pure, spotless church. If we don't start with the right leaders, who can set the compass to the destination of maturity in Christ, we send the church off in failure.

It's as simple as having a good captain at the helm. A successful CEO. A winning coach. As simple as entrusting the church to a man who's already taken his family to the championships.

When we have it, watch out.

So many pastors are extraordinary men with mature families who challenge their congregations to grow in Christ. They are the ones God uses to spark his mission and ignite the church. The rest should follow and learn to be like them.

We have complicated everything.

Privately, many church employees have shared with me they are tempted to leave the ministry not because of personal failure, but church politics.

Yet it should all be about ministry. Not immaturity among church leadership. God's plan is simple. It's about men and women who come wanting to grow. It's about growing them.

That's what's on the line here. Are we willing to sacrifice the spiritual lives of Christians for the status quo?

Godly men with successful "teams" need to stand up and lead the church. To mark the way. Its future depends on them.

But God's Word must be the standard. It would be unwise for us to supplant the commands of God for the traditions of men.

A SIMPLE VISION

God has a beautiful, enchanting Bride he prepares for a wedding day. She catches his eye. He holds his breath. He entrusts her to servants, like Esther, who treat her with oils and ointments and bring her to spotless perfection in anticipation of that day. He chooses men who are faithful with little in their families to transform her into a shimmering Beauty in his church.

We should take this seriously. Paul warns Timothy, "Do not be hasty in the laying on of hands, and do not share in the sins of others. Keep yourself pure" (1 Tim. 5:22).

Paul isn't talking about praying over people. He isn't recommending Timothy hold off from healing sinners. He's talking about empowerment. He says, *don't be hasty and entrust these tasks to the wrong men, laying hands of commission on them*. Otherwise, Timothy will share in their sins. He should keep himself pure from this stain. It rests on him.

And now it rests on us.

God has a design he planned for his church and the godly men he intends to lead it. It's simple. It's revolutionary. It's based upon a code he placed deep in the heart of man. In the next chapter, we will look at how to empower what God wrote there long ago.

What he intended from the beginning.

Chapter Fourteen

EXPONENTIATING THE KINGDOM

I admit it. I was at the mall. A hot summer's day found me in the food court, slurping cold ice water, and talking with friends. Support for a local Christian business had stirred up the Christian community and much of the church from our area came out.

Angela, six-week-old Luke, and I planted ourselves at a table near the fountain in the middle of the court, close enough to the action to watch the day's events unfold.

While I relaxed to trickling sounds and drew sips from refreshing coldness as it clinked in my cup, a couple guys and I struck up a conversation.

The first excitedly told us about the prominent Christian leader whose church he'd attended for more than a decade...and *had* his friend heard of him?

Of course.

What a joy it was to learn under such an anointed leader in a powerful ministry. It had been much trouble finding another who measured up.

They just don't make leaders like that anymore.

"Well, you should be able to take up his place. You learned under him," I joked, slapping him on the back.

Sensing the play, his friend smirked, "That's right."

The man grew silent. Head bowed a little.

"Yeah, well, I haven't really been strong in my faith lately. That's why I'm hoping my wife will get me back into things with this new program she's doing."

I sat there stunned. An awkward silence hung over the three of us.

He knew he was off-track, yet hoped his wife would get him back into his faith?

Though surprised by the passivity, I was struck by something far deeper.

You see, my new friend had just espoused the wonders of learning under an eminent, powerful leader for *over a decade.* A man for whom he could not find a replacement. But the exact goal of the ministry—to disciple followers—had not produced its result in him.

Although he was clearly impressed with it, is it possible the ministry missed something?

Paul pleads, "I urge you to imitate me" (1 Cor. 4:16). In the same letter, he repeats, "Be imitators of me, just as I also am of Christ" (1 Cor. 11:1).

The instructions to imitate Paul are God's clue to how this should work. Paul wants to duplicate everything he is as a disciple of Christ in us. That is discipleship, making followers like the leader—like Christ. It is the goal of ministry.

The extent it does *this* is the extent it is a great ministry. And from that standpoint, as a church, we've got serious work to do.

A NEW CHURCH STRUCTURE

If every man is designed by God with the nature of a leader in him, then something is wrong with the church. In most, a few men lead. The majority are uninvolved. Yet every man's design is masculinity, engineered to produce the same result. Authority. Initiative. Leadership. Strength.

Sadly, this makes the church a horribly inefficient organization. And it's the lives of the saints.

But a man will lead when he knows he is called. It is my belief he will take part when the one he is asked to play fits. As CEO, as general, as pastor of his home—as man—he fits. He has a purpose, not a place in the pew.

He has passion and a mission. It isn't in the armchair.

He has a calling on his life. It isn't at the office.

He has numbers to crunch, deadlines to meet, and clients to win. They are in his little congregation at home.

They will grow, shine, mature, like any church, if he leads them as purposefully as any pastor. Bible in his hand, fire in his heart, he is ordained to take the land. It's time to assemble his team with vision, disciple them with passion, and lead them in the mission.

Like a mighty man.

It's an exciting life. And it begins now.

At least it will, at any rate, when we see every man this way—through the lens of his design, focused sharply on his purpose. The deepest longings of men's hearts will be fulfilled. They will fit. They'll want to be in church.

There's no reason to check out when their presence doesn't add to the church head count; it *shapes* the church. When the part fits who God made them to be, which is leaders of men.

That's God's perspective. When as a society we see it, we'll change.

If everything in God's Word about masculinity's design and purpose is true, a shift needs to occur in church.

And it does.

For a more efficient church with broader scope, the traditional, do-it-yourself, one-man pastor role must change.

It's the only way to empower a much larger church.

THE PLAN

Dad was an excellent coach. Besides studying and learning from the best, he recognized how to coach a team. He understood for the team to be great he couldn't be "the guy."

That's one of the problems with church today. Pastors have a burning desire to make an impact, so they teach. They minister up front. They give the sermons. They lead. They do what needs to be done. It isn't selfish; it's a well-intended desire for an important role. However, if pastors hope to lead a church to make disciples of all nations, it is completely wrong.

Henry Ford, inventor and founder of the Ford Motor Company, famously elevated others to leadership positions rather than performing them himself. It freed him up to do what he found much more valuable—think.

My dad coached the same way. Had he simply tackled the job, we would have remained a mediocre team. Instead, he assembled a staff. He hired assistants with specialty skills. He reached out to former wrestlers willing to coach for little or no pay. He gave official coach's shirts with personalized names and a spot in the coach's chair during matches in exchange for committing to attend practice once a week.

We ended up with the largest staff in the county. Six coaches, sometimes more, arrayed in red coaching shirts lined the mats at our competitions. Each weekend, the two official assistants took the varsity team to a tournament. My dad, the *head coach*, along with the volunteer coaches, took the JV team to another varsity tournament. Most of our 40-50 wrestlers competed and received personalized instruction each week.

The crucial element was Dad understood as a coach he could only do so much. But as an *empowerer* of other coaches, his potential, and the team's, became unlimited. Assistants led practices. They gave inspirational team speeches. They strategized and taught moves. Dad encouraged the wrestlers and gave a coach's corner talk every practice, but often worked in the back preparing and scheduling. He set up a system that empowered other men to lead, which freed him to do what was far more valuable—think. In response, the team's success shot through the roof.

The key to Dad's team and Henry Ford's company was they were both organizations too large for one man to effectively lead. They knew success must be bigger than them.

In most churches, pastors, like most coaches, do the job. They have a small pastoral staff, which isn't nearly enough to equip the entire church. It's enough to effectively run a couple events a week, not grow people to maturity. Unfortunately, such a system doesn't accomplish its purpose of discipling the saints. Yet it rests above a wealth of leadership potential created for that very thing—the men. Still, many pastors don't see their purpose as *empowering* disciples rather than personally running and teaching a church. So their effect is limited.

Like most coaches, they don't know how to build a championship program.

CLUES TO THE SOLUTION

In business, however, this principle is understood well.

There's a reason McDonald's is a multi-billion dollar, world-wide company. It has created a system in which one can follow an exact pattern and be successful. It's simple enough anyone can do it. Because anyone can, they do, and McDonald's makes a lot of money.

I'm not saying the church needs to franchise. Franchises are usually rigidly controlled at the top. I believe too much control hinders good leaders. But there's an important principle of discipleship we should recognize here.

I once ran a business in a global company that provides the clue. It has "systems" of distributors throughout the U.S. and in other countries. The company holds conferences during the year. At one of these regional conferences, I met the company's big guns. Rob (whose name I've changed) shared how he makes $70,000 a month. His story and success are mind-blowing.

Rob leads a local system in his hometown. Every Tuesday evening they meet for 45 minutes to present business opportunities to potential associates. One would think Rob leads every meeting—he speaks at the regional conferences. Surely, everyone would join the business if Rob presented each week.

The reverse is actually true. He rarely speaks. The success of the business is predicated on being duplicable. If it appears only Robs can build big businesses, no one will try. So the system makes success as simple as possible. Then the system empowers people to be leaders.

And the company is brilliant at this. A new leader goes from giving his testimonial about the product to presenting half the slide show during a meeting. Each job progresses until one is responsible for equipment, offering trainings, and coaching new leaders as an expert business owner in the company. The company doesn't simply hope people will become leaders, it *institutionalizes* empowering them.

You see, for the company to be successful, Rob as "the guy" isn't enough; it needs tens of thousands of people to be Robs. If he builds a business, its success relies on him alone. If he helps others build businesses, who help others build businesses, together they can build an empire. Rob can stop at any time because he has trained a system of leaders, not followers.

McDonald's success is predicated on the same thing. The CEO doesn't run his own store. He empowers *others* to run stores effectively. And business exponentiates.

The church, however, is great at building customers. Followers. They sit in pews every Sunday. Unfortunately, it's poor at building leaders. In fact, it's cut all the leaders out. There isn't any place for them.

And, as Terry Moore stated, "When natural leaders walk into a place where there are no opportunities to lead, they naturally leave."

So they launch businesses or build skyscrapers or sit on the couch and watch Sunday Night Football. Far from the church and their true purpose. But leadership is what the church was *designed for*. It wasn't fashioned to win converts. It was created to make disciples.

When Jesus handed the church to his followers, he specifically instructed them, "Go therefore and make disciples of all the nations, baptizing them in the name of the Father and the Son and the Holy Spirit, teaching them to observe all that I commanded you" (Matt. 28:18).

A true disciple doesn't learn something new and go about his business. He does exactly what his mentor does. Like the one who taught him, he teaches and disciples.

Do you see how men's nature was designed to facilitate this? To duplicate the church? God's plan fits perfectly with our natures.

It is my belief, however, that it's the church that does not fit.

In the current church, there is literally no way for believers to "go and do likewise." If they are discipled and taught, there's no systemic place for them to do the same; the structure of the church doesn't allow it.

We hinder our own call by the way we run the modern-day church. 1 Corinthians tells us, "When you come together, everyone has a hymn, or word of instruction, a revelation, a tongue or an interpretation. All of these must be done for the strengthening of the church" (14:26).

Members significantly contributed, which shows empowering the body was important to the early church. Think how on-fire we'd be if everyone becomes a mother or father in the faith. We hope it happens, but have no logical way to bring it about. The church needs to be set up with the systematic goal of forming leaders into more effective leaders and men and women into more mature men and women of God.

First, there must be a plan. Leadership needs to be clear and duplicable. It must be a system that builds ordinary people into leaders. A system whose success is based on their success as leaders, not on one leader's organization. McDonald's and 100 billion served.

Like in Rob's company, the perspective must change from growing one business to growing many. That's when a pastor becomes a successful pastor. Not when he has built a big business. When he has helped countless others build big businesses. That's the "business" of the church. When he does this, the church becomes immeasurable, like the sand of the sea shore, like the stars of the sky. And it grows long after he's gone.

The truth is if Rob gave every presentation at the local meeting, he would have a weak and dying system. A thriving one has scores of leaders sharing, presenting, and developing. They all build thriving businesses. Rob disciples them from behind the scenes and takes the stage for the big conferences to speak to all the leaders. Only on special occasions does Rob speak at the local system.

It's a model that could drastically change the church.

THE PASTOR AND THE PIPELINE

In his book *Rich Dad, Poor Dad*, Robert Kiyosaki explains this principle further. He gives an example of two people who work to supply towns with water. The first carries buckets to the town. It is long, hard work with little reward. The town receives water immediately, but only in small quantities when buckets arrive. The other builds a pipeline. For a while, no water comes. The pipeline is under construction. But once it is finished, the pipeline supplies water to the town in endless quantity with or without the builder's presence. He is no longer necessary. The purpose of supplying water has been accomplished. And it continues long after he's gone. In contrast, the impact of the person who carries buckets ends the moment the last bucket is set down.

That is the problem with the church.

Most pastors carry buckets. They lead in all the crucial ways for the church. They are "the guy." They do the job.

It's a valiant effort. They help people. But they're carrying buckets, rather than building pipelines.

And their impact ends the moment their last sermon is over.

That's why many men, like my new acquaintance in the food court, leave ministries relatively unchanged, looking for the next place to attend on Sunday.

A church with that structure is a church that lacks vision. Unfortunately, it lacks impact. And I have trouble thinking of churches that break out of this mold.

In Mark, Jesus tells a story of seed that fell on different kinds of soil. Some fell on the path, some on rocks, and some among thorns, but some of the seed fell on good soil. He explains, "it came up, grew, and produced a crop, multiplying thirty, sixty, or even a hundred times."

The pastor who carries buckets makes a difference. He plants seed in the soil and grows the people he can. The pastor who builds a pipeline multiplies it a hundred times.

If he does the work himself, like most coaches, he misses the point. He can build something incredible and impact lives long after he's gone if he empowers many others to do it better than he ever could.

This idea changes everything. It's what Jesus did.

He said, "I tell you the truth, anyone who has faith in me will do what I have been doing. He will do even greater things than these, because I am going to the Father" (John 14:12).

Jesus built a pipeline.

He knew he had to step back and hand the ministry to the disciples. The shocking thing was he knew they would do greater things than him. His Spirit would live in them; they were not greater than Jesus. But they would do greater things because he'd work through them, and together the body of disciples could do much more than he could alone. They would multiply themselves and their disciples would multiply and exponentiate the kingdom and its power. Jesus wasn't overly spiritual, pretending they couldn't do his ministry as well as him. He told them they would do it and more.

Jesus mentored twelve for that purpose. When he sent them out in twos to cast out demons, preach, teach, and heal, what do you think he was doing? He was handing over the kingdom to them, little by little, while he remained with them. He had them practice while he could disciple them in it. Later, it would be completely in their hands.

He built a pipeline, and he empowered leaders.

Are we ready to follow Jesus?

A successful church doesn't have one pastor; it has a hundred. Each isn't called pastor. That's redundant and, in our culture, showy. But the head pastor shifts the perspective from his ministry alone. His job is to empower everyone else's.

And look who he has to lead alongside him—every other man. They've been bred for the job. In the context of church leadership, every man has been outfitted with the nature of a leader. And if they lead faithfully, they bring everyone—man and woman—into action.

For this perspective to influence the church, it starts with the pastor.

Like my dad and Henry Ford, he may no longer be "the guy." His job is to build up other men as leaders and empower everyone in the Body. He may still give sermons, but he recognizes his role as a leader of leaders is more important. He gives fewer. More men are apprenticed into that. He leads fewer Bible studies. Other men do that. The more they follow him through his daily interactions the better, being mentored by his insights as the disciples were by Jesus.

Like Rob in the business, he takes a global approach. He doesn't present every meeting. He builds behind the scenes.

And the church thrives with activity as other men sharpen their skills. The pastor builds a pipeline; it takes growth. It takes time. Little will be seen while the pipes are being laid. But after it is finished, it supplies water to thousands without any effort from him. He goes on, apprenticing and empowering others as he has the first.

Multiplying a hundred times.

Let's not be overly spiritual about our roles, as Jesus wasn't. When one dies, would one rather have given sermons every Sunday and brought many to Christ? Or have built a team that created tens or hundreds of leaders who brought thousands or tens of thousands to Christ and matured them as disciples? Over the years, that is the impact of this perspective on ministry.

Sure, creating vision and setting a team foundation wasn't as personally satisfying for Dad as teaching a few moves to kids on the floor. But the wisdom to build what he did instead was far more valuable. And it became incredibly satisfying to him in the long run. With this model, he created a championship team.

Is personally doing the work really that important?

If a pastor needs more motivation, he should look to God himself, who made the same choice by entrusting the keys of the kingdom to the church.

WORSHIP PASTORS AND THE PIPELINE

Many worship leaders focus on building the perfect team. It's easier to control the results. But consequently, they're always struggling to maintain the team, and they don't have a constant pipeline of musicians. It's the wrong strategy for a worship program.

That's the reason our wrestling team sent two full squads of wrestlers to varsity tournaments. Had we only filled one lineup, the team would've adapted to that size. And the growth of the wrestlers who didn't compete would've been stunted.

The same is true in worship. Think of the musicians whose talents are wasted in church if there is only one worship team instead of three. There's no place to develop. No feeder system.

In wrestling, our second squad was a pipeline for the varsity team of another complete line-up of wrestlers with significant varsity experience. And others were trained to fill *their* spots.

Similarly, the worship leader should forget the goal of one excellent team and immediately begin from the concept of two or more teams, *no matter how many musicians he has.* Even with a few, if he can find two who are musically strong and competent to lead, he should empower them to find and train their own musicians. Skip every other pew and you'll find those who play or want to learn. It's opportunities that are few. Raise up two or three leaders, and instrumentalists will attract to the ministry. Build one team of the best, and the ministry will shrink to the size of that team, always struggling to maintain it.

There can even be a beginner team that plays at the youth group or informal functions. Expand the pipeline by empowering leaders and ministry will flourish. The vision makes the difference.

In whatever ministry, a limited vision creates a small team and values "excellence" over empowerment. A broad one reaches out, empowers, and ends up with pipelines of capable, qualified servants.

But one problem in worship, as well as pastoring, is the struggle to release the ministry to others. Worship pastors began, most likely, because they want to play. It's easy to miss their role in the kingdom beyond their craft. They have to let go of doing it themselves to empower. That is Christ's vision for a leader as discipleship occurs.

An effective worship pastor has 3-5 leaders he is grooming at all times to do his job. A wise plan would be at least three worship leaders with their own full teams. Like the pastor, he rarely leads himself. He coaches and empowers other leaders for success. To build a championship program.

He oversees. He disciples leaders. Each of the 3-5 worship leaders mentors and trains the musicians in his team to eventually do his job, just as the worship pastor does.

And they do it with *purpose*.

This is a church with a global vision that will impact nations. It will exponentiate, as Jesus intended it to do at its inception.

A CULTURE OF LEADERS

As this occurs, a culture of leadership grows. The reason no one steps up in most churches, I hate to say, is because pastors have created a culture in which no one is expected to. All expectations rest on them, so people begin to believe no one else can do the job as well. And they never will until the paradigm changes. But it's the wrong mindset. It's a result of pastors leading alone, and it's the exact opposite culture they want to grow.

Instead, pastors should look to bring every man into the pipeline of leadership (and all men and women into the pipeline of ministry). Those who aren't mature follow and grow; those ready for responsibility or authority receive it. The pastor assesses each to find the right place in discipleship. At the appropriate maturity level, they progress to the next step.

The system creates the disciples. The pastor facilitates it.

This isn't about merely getting people involved, but maturing and empowering effective leaders.

The leaders then mature and empower everyone else.

Women are essential in this. God calls them to lead other women, lead children, and use their gifts to enrich the entire church. Effective leadership provides women's passions and abilities the place to flourish. They are vital. Each is brought into the pipeline as it widens.

Watch the church take off when we understand this vision. It will be awesome to behold. When everyone is fully involved and strong in the Lord, we will certainly do "greater things than these."

THE CHANGE AND ITS ENEMY

One important aspect of this—it is my belief—is every person in ministry should be training multiple people to take over his job. Like the worship leader, the pastor should have 3-5 men at all times who are ready to step in and become the next pastor or be sent out to pastor.

Every church has many men who are mature in Christ. The pastor picks a number of these. They are each qualified based on a well-managed family at home. He apprentices them as Jesus did.

These men, as well as others being trained to take *their* spots, may give sermons, lead Bible studies, make announcements, organize events, do home visits, and perform any pastoral duties alongside or in place of the head pastor. He sets this up as he sees fit to strengthen the church.

Yet, the church must be given this vision. They have to understand the church is a ministry that empowers leaders.

If the pastor shares this new vision with the church, it will catch fire. Men and women dream about joining a mission. The pastor invites them into one.

Meanwhile, he actively builds his team of mature, godly men. He chooses appropriate roles and duties that lead them in sequentially taking over his position.

Yes, I said that right. Many pastors are afraid of someone taking their power or position away. Some worry other men will threaten their leadership. So they hoard it like a man who buries his mina in the ground and, like him who tries to hold onto his life, they lose it.

But that misses the point of pastoral success. A pastor *only becomes successful* when other men in his church have as much or greater success than he does. It's the same as a father wanting his son to be a better man than him. That is discipleship, and it is explicitly the goal of the ministry.

It is the change that is necessary in the church, and its enemy is control.

I understand the temptation. Every pastor has been hurt. Every one has had men strive for power and deceptively try to snatch his ministry away, or at least manipulate it.

It's similar to a woman who has been hurt by an ex-boyfriend. The immediate temptation is to close her heart and decide never to trust again. She builds walls to protect herself, but they only imprison her.

The pastor who closes his ministry off to other men's influence is no different. It's too risky to trust. So he builds walls to keep them away. Ironically, they imprison him, separating him from support by a wide moat—the pastor gap. This distances him from his real purpose, discipling the men he's called to make like him.

Could you imagine if Jesus hadn't trusted his disciples? He might have avoided being betrayed by Judas. But he'd never have experienced John resting on his breast or walking the journey with his brothers. The ones who desperately needed to experience it with him. For soon, he'd leave them the church.

Are we getting how crucial this is?

Hoarding power or position is not godly leadership. The wise, godly leader gives it away. Not foolishly or to the wrong men. But to appropriate men he appropriates the right amount of responsibility to build them into effective leaders who lead long after he's gone. He is through carrying buckets. He builds a pipeline. And the more the pipeline widens, the more he multiplies his ministry.

Even a hundred times.

Like my mom said, "I think possibly the greatest witness is when strong men in the church can co-exist and not be threatened by each others' strength."

Some leaders are afraid another will take their job. The godly view of leadership is constantly looking for the men who will replace them.

Then they've done what McDonald's has done. What Henry Ford and his team of employees accomplished. What my dad with our wrestling team achieved. And what Jesus did.

They've built a team that could change the world.

It's the Great Commission.

When they've given it away many times over, then, and only then, they've done their job.

-*Chapter Fifteen*-
LEADER OF MEN

The squeeze of the trigger felt good under my finger. Sharp pops pierced the air as the sheet beyond me peppered with a tight cluster of holes. The smell of gunpowder filled my nostrils.

It was a nice grouping.

Here we were—Dad, the boys, and the family lever action Henry rifle.

This was no ordinary weapon. It was a gift from my brother Doy to Dad and the brothers.

The rifle was a thing of beauty. Gold-plated, wood-grained; it was no stock firearm, but a marquee weapon from a manufacturer trusted to make American rifles since the Wild West.

And in the shiny stock, so thoughtfully chosen, were the words engraved: "Mister, you ever seen what a Henry rifle can do in the hands of someone that knows how to use it?"

As I said, this was no ordinary firearm.

It was a symbol, an icon from our favorite "Demsick classic" cowboy movie—*Silverado.* In one scene, Mal, one of the good guys, confronts a pair of rough riding cattlemen who've bullied his family off the land they own. Cattle now roam it. But Mal has come home. He faces them, unarmed, with a small, withered man riding double behind him and coolly warns the riders if he finds one cow on his land when he returns he's going to start carving steaks.

"And believe me, that's one thing I know about."

Shocked, one of the riders retorts, "Killing cattle is a hanging offense in these parts. If we shot you down right now, we'd be within our rights."

Mal calmly answers—again—unarmed, "Mister, you ever seen what a Henry rifle can do in the hands of someone who knows how to use it?"

Incensed, his assailant roars, "Who would that be? You??"

From behind Mal, a Henry rifle levels directly at them. It is his father's.

The cattle men ride off in a flurry.

This is the moment Doy so thoughtfully captured with his gift and we've all captured out here on the range together, taking turns ratcheting back the lever like cowboys and firing the family token of strength one burst at a time. To us, it's more than a rifle. It is a symbol of the strength of men fully alive—of four brothers and a father who leads them—and the transfer of boldness from him to them.

It is a moment that stirs our blood in the movie.

It is a moment, as I smoothly cock the lever, flicking an empty cartridge into the dirt and loading another into its chamber, that stirs me now.

So, how does a father in the faith disciple another man?

The answer is simple.

He already knows.

He disciples him exactly as he would a son. And as this transfer occurs, moment by moment, he hands him the keys to the kingdom.

A NEW PARADIGM

Dad strategizes and organizes behind the scenes while five coaches train the wrestlers. Henry Ford thinks while other men run the plants. This is a new perspective of leadership and possibly a new standard.

For man's nature to be involved in church, for the transfer of masculine strength to take place, pastors need to change how they think about men.

Each is equipped with the design of authority and strength for the kingdom. When one walks in the door, the pastor sees it written on his forehead. It is written in his DNA.

And the pastor must capture this for the church to be effective.

It isn't enough to be a bearer of buckets. He may no longer merely teach his congregation. He understands he must speak into the twelve, as Jesus did, who will speak into the world. Remember, Jesus hid the mysteries of the kingdom from all but the twelve. When he spoke in parables, he did not do so, as many mistakenly assume, to explain his analogies to his listeners. They do that when one understands. Rather, he did it to *hide* the meanings from those to whom it was not given. He repeatedly says this. However, to the twelve he shared his secrets. And what was "whispered in their ears," they shouted from the mountaintops.

I am not saying pastors should speak cryptically. I am indicating Jesus chose not to only speak to crowds. He built up twelve leaders and specifically poured everything into three. The church was to be built by them.

The twelve spoke into the next generation. Paul also indicated this when he instructed Timothy not to pastor the church of Ephesus, but to *choose* pastors and servant-leaders for the church. There were many. Authority was instilled in them. A system of discipleship characterized the early church.

I wonder if pastors think they would be marginalized if they empowered like this. It may cause them to assume their gifts won't impact people if they pour into disciples. But if pastors shift their purpose to empowering leaders, they won't be silent or unused.

Rob, the business leader, certainly wasn't. He needed to step aside to build a system of successful leaders, but the largest crowd always followed him at meetings. He was the expert. And while the leaders grew in their abilities and influence, his influence grew, as well.

Having pastors empower other leaders won't invalidate them. Actually, it will validate them even more. It won't devalue or minimize their gifts and calling. It will enhance their ministry and usefulness to the kingdom, like it did with Dad for our wrestling team. They'll still use their gifts. But the focus will be on building leaders and, by doing so, building all men and women into mature, empowered Christians. The pastor knows involving leaders in increasing responsibility causes the church to branch out and grow. Causes it to *multiply*.

Rob gave the presentations at the national and regional conferences each year. He was involved in the inner-working of the local system, as well. It just didn't *need him* because of the job he'd done building a pipeline of leaders.

If pastors had this global vision for their ministries, it would have an immeasurable impact on the church. The whole church would buy into the vision of growing many leaders.

It hurts my heart whenever I hear of a church that starts a satellite service and projects the pastor of the main church on the big screen for its sermons. They invalidate every mature Christian man in the congregation. Worse yet, they further institutionalize the problem of eliminating capable leaders by making one man the minister over *additional* churches. Tear down the projector screen and build up a man in its place.

Satellite churches should have satellite pastors. The church will grow when we look for ways to nurture every man's influence rather than extend one man's. That's a plan for church stagnation and death.

It's the result of misguided thinking that focuses on the Sunday morning *experience* rather than maturing effective disciples who are actually discipled to do something.

And a new perspective changes it.

However, I have to admit, I like my pastor. I learn from him. So I'm not especially excited to hear someone else preach. But teach me a purpose of my church is to empower leaders, who are discipled at varying levels of ministry, and everything changes. Now I feel things are happening at my church. It is a place of purpose. I relish hearing other men, knowing they are becoming powerful preachers and leaders. Perhaps someday even I will be one.

Everything hinges on the paradigm—how we *think* about church. Change our perspective and we change how we feel about it. It all starts with training. Teach men and women the reasons and they'll love what they might've opposed. They'll take ownership of the church.

The same is true in the family. Change how we think about men and women and we'll recognize and start to love the differences.

At its core, it occurs to me this is all about masculinity and femininity. Like a Matrix code skittering across a screen, meaning jumps out at us from every line. It transforms how we think about the family and church from the inside.

And the paradigm needs to change to match the church's true purpose.

A CRISIS OF IMAGE: BRIDGING THE PASTOR GAP

As it changes, the church begins to grow. Men and women are engaged, living as God designed them. The institution builds leaders as a natural byproduct of its discipleship, and they are empowered. No longer does it alienate them at arm's length. The pastor gap—between the pastor and congregation—begins to close.

This is only possible if the pastor's style of ministry isn't maintaining power and control, but enabling and empowering. His vision creates or kills the growth.

Once we recognize the common thread in men of leadership in the family and church, the common DNA, the common purpose, we see there shouldn't be a gap at all. The head pastor leads the church. He disciples the other men to be leaders like him. Yet he is one of them. A body of leaders all working together under his authority. He should be purposeful about establishing that closeness. For, "behold how good and pleasant it is for brothers to dwell together in unity" (Psalm 133:1, NASB).

Such pastors empower men in their churches as a father does a son. Such men empower their wives and children as Christ does a Beloved.

Yet, another hindrance stands in the way of growing a successful community of leadership. It is more insidious than control. It is sneaky. It creeps in and masquerades as wisdom, a good witness; but it is worldly and self-serving at its core. Similar to control, it is based on fear, not love. And, if unchecked, it will destroy fellowship and camaraderie in a community of leaders.

It is the temptation to protect one's image.

Pride causes us to want to look better than we are. It may be tempting to appear perfect before the church, but when a pastor tries to protect his image it halts the growth of a community of leaders. He must open up to real, honest accountability and friendship with his brothers. Otherwise, he sets himself up as something above it. Honestly, that's unholy. God doesn't want him to be separate from the others, be better, or worse yet, *appear* better. Paul didn't hesitate to come "in weakness and fear, and with much trembling" (1 Cor. 2:31).

Men can grow in leadership if the pastor has the humility to show them how a godly man walks the journey. He needs to be real enough to model how a good leader responds to his own weakness, fear, and sin. How will they ever deal with these temptations when they get to his position if he hasn't discipled them by his own example? How can they do it now?

Together, men bear each other's burdens. They are cut from the same cloth. They follow the same Lion, Jesus. And they need to see the pastor glorify God as the lion he is, not a paper lion, an illusion.

Image-based leaders create cultures of image-based Christianity. I've seen it many times. Eventually people are alienated by their own mirrors, distanced by their walls, and the community of leadership becomes shallow and fake. It ironically becomes the immature faith it intends to appear to avoid.

Christ chose character.

It is real, genuine. It does not care about reputation. Its witness is not based on fear of what others think or do, but the courage to be different. It is bold and public. It braves the opinions of the crowd, the hypocrite, and the gossip.

And it is incredibly attractive to the world.

Truthfully, I have found the more one hides one's spots and blemishes, the more one becomes superficial. Image-based mindsets always produce fakeness. Character is the antithesis to this. One can either invest in image or invest in character, never both.

Look at Christ. He never cared how he looked, only how he acted.

He didn't mince words with the church of his day, the Pharisees, nor bend when they wouldn't listen. He lived a radical, counter-culture life to the world. He could have been a more compliant Messiah and casually gone about fitting in, but he wouldn't have been the Father's.

And he wouldn't have made a difference.

One can't minister to sinners, on their level, without getting a little dirty. One can't live in authentic relationships in the church without being real.

If we go this route as men, together, we will never go wrong. In any setting, the more we choose character over image, the more we become men of character. The more we choose the reverse, the more we compromise. Paper lions. Men of image. Not lions like the Lion of Judah.

It is one of the more valuable truths, this sliding scale.

Jesus made his choice clear.

He was rejected by men. A man of sorrows. He was called a glutton and a drunkard for eating meals with sinners and drinking wine with prostitutes. He ignored the critics. Said leave them. They are blind guides.

In the church, we often pander. We put nice, indirect Bible references on it, but our pat answers don't fit who Jesus was. They compromise truth by ignoring the whole of Scripture. As we follow this pattern, we find ourselves focused more and more on image, on how we look as Christians and as leaders. And we call it holiness. But image is indeed a sliding scale away from true holiness. Jesus would have none of it.

In so many ways, he specifically chose to let the accusers in the church of his day see his spots. He welcomed it. He healed in front of them on the Sabbath. He challenged the leaders' popular interpretations of Scripture. He dared them to throw stones and prove sinless. He made friends with sinners and chose their company over the elite. He chose character over image.

There are people whose company we are not to share. It isn't sinners. It is Christians who pervert the Word and won't repent. *Don't even eat with them and let their compromise influence you*, Paul cautions. Jesus ate and drank with sinners, but not in sin. He honored God in a way they had never seen before. He lifted up the cup. With what we often call unholy, he glorified the Father. He didn't party or lead anyone into sin. He prayed with it, made it holy. Image says don't tread on these topics. Put down the cup. Pussyfoot around the hard issues and be a good example to the flock. Live to a higher standard.

My standard will not supersede my Savior's.

In a strange, yet powerful way, Jesus takes these topics that no one will tackle and makes them new. He raises them before the Father, blesses him, and transforms them in the presence of an unbelieving world. A world in awe.

He rejects the superficiality of image and the allure of men's approval, even the approval of the church, and he embraces truth, transforming the perception of it before their eyes. He is not afraid to be "rejected by men" if he must. He chooses what is right, no matter how it looks, and redefines to a world the meaning it so desperately needs. To be transformed.

Pastors, would you lead us in this? I've heard of so many pastors compromising the Word on controversial topics because the politics of their churches won't accept what they believe. Pandering cripples the churches they are meant to grow. Forget the critics. Disciple them or leave them. Jesus did. The worst they can do is crucify you next to him. Will you lead us in being bold as lions?

As William Wallace said in *Braveheart*, "If you would just lead them…they'd follow you. And so would I."

Lead us in genuine faith. Show us how to unreservedly and honestly be a leader without hiding imperfections, without covering spots or avoiding critics, so we can follow.

A generation of men will be spared the tortures of alienation in church ministry if we pass this along now. And perhaps generations that follow.

Show us how to value character over image. Open up to us so we can make the journey with you.

Show us how to be leaders of men.

BREATHING OUT

When all men become leaders in some capacity, a funny thing happens. The pressure comes off the pastor. He no longer has to do it alone. All men take responsibility and the system is built for the transfer of increasing responsibility to them. The pastor becomes the head of a true community of brothers who are one in the mission.

One like Christ and the Father are one.

There's a lot of support that can be taken from a team. Pastors burn out or seriously consider leaving the ministry because they often perform it in an unnatural manner. It's unhealthy for the weight of the church to rest on any one man's shoulders but Christ. With a web of leaders, the pastor is held up. He is rejuvenated and re-inspired by their help. They do everything together. The pressure isn't on him, because many men bear the burden of the church. He coaches, protects, observes, strategizes, and leads its overall health. But the other men are the hands and feet of the leadership team. They lead with him and directly minister to the people.

The pastor can breathe out.

There's no burnout when there's no overload.

No grand questioning of purpose or life direction. There's no eye on the door, quietly coaxing him to leave the ministry.

The truth is the pastor was never meant to do it alone.

He's one of many. One of a brotherhood.

I think of DNA. I think of nature. If pastors who are dying to maintain ministries that are slowly killing them understood their brothers were cut from the same cloth, called, even *designed* for it, they would breathe easier.

They wouldn't be falling under the pressure. They wouldn't be struggling alone.

They would be in a community of leaders.

It's time we knew these heroes who've fought so hard for the faith are meant to be joined by a whole army. An insurmountable throng, one worthy of Jesus himself saying, "[You] will do even greater things than these" (John 14:12). Greater than one man.

Greater than the One.

God knew these things from the beginning. He saw how everything would fit together perfectly, how it would be "very good."

He saw what we could not—how the interlocking pieces of the design would match up so complexly, so marvelously, they would reveal the splendor of his crowning creation.

Man and woman.

He saw how the revelation of glory would culminate at the moment each piece ascends to its natural place to form his most breathtaking beauty of all, his Bride.

Christ and the church.

So simple, so natural. So undeniably freeing.

Like breathing in and breathing out.

ACKNOWLEDGMENTS

I'm deeply grateful—thank you God. You make my dreams come true one grain of sand at a time.

Thank you, Dad. I have learned nearly every good thing I know from you. Whole chapters of this book were written from your life. You are a man of God I am honored to follow. I love you.

Thank you, Mom. You are a true woman of God who epitomizes femininity—to Dad and to the world. You are the best example of a wife and mom a guy could have. I love you.

I am also deeply indebted to my three brothers: Robert, Doy, and Richard. Being together in our little army sharpened us. You are men I've been proud to laugh and cry alongside, worship and bleed with. Men I hope are closer than best friends all my life. You sharpen me still.

Thank you to all my friends. Special thanks to Terry Moore, a kindred warrior with the same heart for discipleship, and Bart Wise, my mentor, whose adventurer spirit is inspiring.

I am extremely grateful to Bill Proctor for his insightful critique. Additionally, many thanks to the launch team who have dedicated their time to make this project successful.

But I would be a fool to leave out the one person who has put up with all this. I love you, green eyes. You are the love of my life. Thank you, My Amazing.

WHAT YOU CAN DO

Thank you for joining this adventure. If you have been impacted by this book or inspired along the way and want to help spread the message of the beauty of masculinity and femininity and how it can transform marriages, families, and churches, please consider doing one or all of the following:

- Write a quick review on Amazon.com
- Send a brief tweet or social media post telling your friends they won't want to miss this book
- Tell your friends personally why they'll want to read it
- Give the book to a friend
- Contact John-Peter Demsick to speak at your church's event (JPDemsick@gmail.com, @JPDemsick on Twitter)

But most of all, consider taking one simple--yet hard--infinitely crucial step: live it.

And Breathe. A little in. A deep one out. It's what you were born to do...

ABOUT THE AUTHOR

John-Peter Demsick is an author, songwriter, and inspirational speaker. He lives in Vero Beach, Florida with his wife, Angela, and son, Luke. Angela is pregnant with their daughter.

John-Peter has served in various capacities in church leadership for fifteen years (and taught English for eight), and currently serves at St. Paul's Church in Vero Beach as assistant youth director and youth worship leader.

His passions include surfing, breakdancing, songwriting, screenwriting, and living near the ocean—closer to "the edge of the world." His dream is to sail the world with his family, teaching them Latin and the atlas, seeing nothing but blue in every direction, his kids with frayed Capris and shaggy hair. He has yet to learn Latin.

www.ingramcontent.com/pod-product-compliance
Lightning Source LLC
Chambersburg PA
CBHW031346040426
42444CB00005B/205